James K. Polk

United States Presidents

James K. Polk

Series Consultant:
Don M. Coerver, professor of history
Texas Christian University, Forth Worth, Texas

Alison Davis Tibbitts

Enslow Publishers, Inc.

44 Fadem Road   PO Box 38
Box 699   Aldershot
Springfield, NJ 07081   Hants GU12 6BP
USA   UK
http://www.enslow.com

Dedication

For my mother, Helen, and her father, Edward,
who taught me to travel the world through the written word.

Library of Congress Cataloging-in-Publication Data

Tibbitts, Alison
    James K. Polk / Alison Davis Tibbitts.
      p. cm. — (United States presidents)
    Includes bibliographical references and index.
    Summary: A biography of the eleventh president, who previously
served as a U.S. congressman and governor of Tennessee.
    ISBN 0-7660-1037-6
    1. Polk, James K. (James Knox), 1795–1849—Juvenile literature.
    2. Presidents—United States—Biography—Juvenile literature.
    3. United States—Politics and government—1845–1849—Juvenile
literature. [1. Polk, James K. (James Knox), 1795–1849.
    2. Presidents. 3. United States—Politics and government—1845–1849.]
    I. Title. II. Series.
    E417.T53 1999
    973.6'1'092
    [B]—DC21   98-29554
                                              CIP
                                              AC

Printed in the United States of America

10 9 8 7 6 5 4 3 2 1

To Our Readers:
All Internet addresses in this book were active and appropriate when we went to press. Any comments or suggestions can be sent by e-mail to Comments@enslow.com or to the address on the back cover.

Illustration Credits: *American Advertising Posters of the Nineteenth Century* (New York: Dover Publications, Inc., 1976), p. 59; Casey Tibbitts, San Diego, Calif., p. 15; Courtesy of George Eastman House, p. 101; Courtesy of U. S. Naval Academy Archives, p. 103; Enslow Publishers, Inc., pp. 39, 67, 82, 93; James K. Polk Memorial Association, Columbia, Tenn., pp. 11, 20, 23; National Archives and Records Administration, Washington, D.C., p. 92; San Diego Historical Society, Photograph Collection, p. 94; Tennessee State Library and Archives, Nashville, Tenn., pp. 6, 21, 43, 105, 113; Tennessee State Museum, Nashville, Tenn., pp. 9, 30; *War and Conflict*, National Archives, Washington, D.C., pp. 66, 85, 89, 90, 91.

All of the following were reproduced from *The Dictionary of American Portraits*, published by Dover Publications, Inc., in 1967:
Daguerreotype by Mathew Brady. Courtesy Library of Congress, p. 75; Engraved by W. J. Edwards from a daguerreotype by Mathew Brady, p. 56; Painting by Edward Schnabel. Courtesy Gregory's Old Master Gallery, p. 40; Painting by Paul L' Ouvrier. Courtesy New York Historical Society, p. 38

Source Document Credits:
Library of Congress, pp. 41, 70, 71.

Cover Illustration: James K. Polk Memorial Association, Columbia, Tenn.

Contents

George Peter Alexander Healy painted this portrait of Polk early in his term as the eleventh president of the United States.

1
INAUGURATION DAY

James Polk gazed out the window of his room at the National Hotel. In the pale morning light, he saw neither the raindrops bouncing along the street below nor the wintry landscape of bare trees against a leaden sky. His attention was focused on the start of a long-awaited, hard-won day. It was March 4, 1845. Before nightfall, James Knox Polk would become the eleventh president of the United States.

Polk and his wife, Sarah, had been in Washington, D.C., since mid-February. Many family members and friends had come with them, traveling seven hundred miles from Tennessee by horseback, stagecoach, steamboat, and train. People in towns and villages all along the way had come out to greet Polk and his party and wish them well.

Washington's residents ignored the steady rainfall as they hurried to the Capitol for the inauguration ceremony. Lines of carriages lurched along the unpaved roads, splashing through potholes and puddles as they entered the grounds surrounding the building. Foreign ministers in gold-braided uniforms dashed toward the Senate chamber and the welcoming warmth inside.

At exactly 11:00 A.M., President John Tyler arrived at the National Hotel to collect the president-elect. Tradition required that the outgoing and incoming presidents ride together in an open carriage along Pennsylvania Avenue to the Capitol in full view of the people. Cannons thundered and church bells chimed across the city to celebrate the historic day.[1]

Sarah Polk, wearing a stylish blue velvet cloak and bonnet, waited with friends for her husband to reach the Capitol. Samuel F. B. Morse, the American artist and inventor, sat near her chair. Morse held on his lap the new electric telegraph machine he had invented a year earlier. He planned to tap his descriptions of unfolding events into the device and transmit them to newspapers fifty miles away in Baltimore, Maryland.[2]

Polk watched as the vice-president-elect, George Mifflin Dallas, took his oath of office in the Senate chamber. Afterward, Polk and Dallas joined dignitaries waiting outside at the East Portico of the building. At precisely 12:00 noon, Chief Justice Roger B. Taney of the Supreme Court administered the thirty-five-word oath to James Knox Polk.

Clad in a long, sweeping cape, the brand new forty-nine-year-old president tipped his top hat several times to the cheering crowd before he began his inaugural speech. Former president John Quincy Adams later described the crowd assembled to hear Polk speak as "a large assemblage of umbrellas."[3]

The new president spoke of important national issues. He firmly supported annexation, or incorporation, of the Texas Territory to the United States, an action accomplished by outgoing president Tyler just three days earlier.

This engraving from the Illustrated London News *shows the new president delivering his inaugural address. The crowd was later described by former president John Quincy Adams as "a large assemblage of umbrellas."*

Polk referred to the long-standing dispute between the United States and Great Britain over the Oregon Territory. The region's northern border had been a major issue in Polk's election campaign. He stated again his belief that America's right to the entire area was "clear and unquestionable."[4]

The president expressed his deep respect and support for every American when he said, "All citizens . . . native or adopted are . . . entitled to equal rights and equal protection."[5] He used the word *happy* a dozen times in the address to describe his hopes for the country's future and for his own term in office.

People lined the streets to applaud the parade that escorted the Polks from the Capitol to the White House. Formally dressed congressmen, foreign diplomats, and Supreme Court justices lent dignity to the review, and brass bands set a brisk pace for military marching units.

The day's celebrations ended with two different events. The first was the official Inaugural Ball, held at the elegant Carusi's Restaurant. Politicians of all parties paid ten dollars per ticket to attend the gala. (It was the first Inaugural Ball ever to make a profit, and the generous sum of one thousand dollars was divided between two Washington orphanages.)

The second party, although not an official event, was held at the National Theater. All who regarded themselves as "pure Democrats" bought two-dollar tickets to attend the festivities there.[6]

Polk's first presidential evening nearly caused an

international embarrassment. The planning committee for the official Inaugural Ball realized too late that they had failed to invite the Diplomatic Corps. Members of this elite group represented foreign governments and royal courts in Washington, and omitting them from the guest list would have been a grave political insult.

When the "pure Democrats" heard about the pending disaster, they invited the diplomats to celebrate with them at the National Theater. Ambassadors and foreign ministers accepted the kind invitation and had a rollicking good time mingling with the tradesmen and shopkeepers. No one said a word when one diplomat's grandly dressed wife danced with her gardener.

Polk commissioned this fan for his wife to commemorate his inauguration as America's eleventh president. Ornate fans were an important accessory for ladies of fashion in the nineteenth century.

Sarah Polk, who had a great interest in fashion, wore a blue-ribboned silk and satin gown fashioned by the famous French designer, Charles Worth. She carried a hand-painted fan that Polk had commissioned especially for her. On one side, it bore miniature portraits of all eleven presidents. Each man's name and position in the presidential roll call was inscribed, and Polk referred to himself as the "president-elect." On the other side of the fan was an image of the Declaration of Independence.

The Polks attended both inaugural balls but spent more time with the Democrats. John Quincy Adams later remarked that the couple "supped with the true blue 2 dollar democracy."[7] They stayed late and enjoyed the party before retiring to spend their first night in the White House.

2

THE COUNTRY BOY

James Polk's ancestors came to America from Ireland in the late 1600s, looking for inexpensive and fertile farmland. James's great-great-grandfather, Robert Bruce Polk, was the first to arrive. He settled in Somerset County, Maryland. Robert's grandson, William, farmed in Pennsylvania before moving to North Carolina in the 1750s.

The Polks adjusted well to life in North Carolina, where the citizens of Mecklenburg County lived by the principles of two great men. One was John Calvin, the founder of Scotland's Presbyterian Church. The other was Thomas Jefferson, America's third president.

The people followed Calvin's strict teachings about God and the Scriptures. They embraced Jefferson's beliefs in ". . . the virtues of the agricultural setting and a simplelife [sic] . . . only peripherally touched by a limited government."[1] Mecklenburg's citizens were said to live ". . . on the fruits of their own labor without expectations of easy wealth. . . ."[2]

The Polks soon became community leaders. In 1775, several men of the family helped prepare the Mecklenburg Resolves. This document was America's first written declaration of independence. Everyone who signed it agreed to cut all his ties with Great Britain.[3]

The Polk clan served honorably in the Revolutionary War, with the exception of James's grandfather. Ezekiel Polk, always a hothead, disobeyed a military order during the war and was stripped of his rank. He had much less interest in independence after that. Ezekiel lived for many years in Mecklenburg County where he built a home near Sugar Creek, married twice, and raised a family.

In 1794, Ezekiel's second son, Samuel, married Jane Knox. She was a great grandniece of John Knox, Scotland's most respected religious and political leader. The couple built a log house on two hundred fifty acres in Pineville, near the border with South Carolina. James Knox Polk arrived at noon on November 2, 1795. He was the first of ten children, six boys and four girls.[4]

James's father, Samuel, was never a regular church-goer. His poor example infuriated the local Presbyterian minister, Reverend James Willis. At James's baptism the preacher refused to begin the ceremony until he had confronted Samuel about his lack of religion. Samuel lost his temper and stormed out of the church with his sobbing wife and unbaptized baby in tow.

Ezekiel and Samuel Polk sometimes worked as surveyors for the military. Their job was to measure the borders, or boundaries, of specified areas. They were paid with either money or parcels of land. Payments in property became final after the previous owners died or moved away. Ownership then passed to the Polks, who could choose to keep the land or to resell it. Samuel occasionally took James on his surveying trips. The boy

This log house in Pineville, North Carolina, is a reconstruction of the one where James Polk was born. The original log house was in ruins by the time Polk became president in 1845.

stayed close to the campfire to care for the horses and help with the cooking.

Over the years, the Polks accumulated a large amount of land. Ezekiel became especially curious about one of his newer properties near the town of Columbia, Tennessee. In 1803, he packed up his immediate family and moved across the mountains to what was known then as the "far west."

Three years later, Samuel and Jane Polk decided that their family should move to Tennessee, too. They traveled five hundred miles through wild and rugged country to the Duck River valley, where they built a log cabin close to Ezekiel's farm. They cleared away tall thickets of grasses and reeds, called canebrake, and planted their first crops of corn and tobacco.

James was frail, and he caught many colds and childhood diseases. He also suffered from chronic stomach upsets and abdominal cramps. He spent hours indoors, resting beside the hearth, while his siblings worked and played outside. When James felt well enough, he played with them, rode his horse, and did his chores. One of his jobs was to cart bags of corn to Micajah Brooks's mill, located ten miles from home, to be ground into meal. Brooks later described James as a ". . . good and faithful mill boy—I . . . turned many a bushel into the hopper that he rode on to my mill."[5]

Jane Polk taught all her children the strict beliefs of her beloved Presbyterian religion. She stressed that people should work hard, accept their lives without complaint, and never waste time. James heard these lessons time and again throughout the years. He gradually became a serious and self-contained child without much confidence or sense of humor.

Despite all their business successes, the Polks worried constantly about James. In 1810, his abdominal pains grew much worse. Local doctors could not find a cause, and the few available medicines did not help. By the age of sixteen, James had become so thin and weak that his parents feared for his life. They decided he must see Dr. Physick, a renowned surgeon who lived eight hundred miles away in Pennsylvania.[6] Samuel rigged up a covered bed on a farm wagon so that his son could lie down during the trip. It was agreed that one of James's uncles would take him to Pennsylvania while his parents stayed at home with the other children.

James, his uncle, and some assistants reached Green River, Kentucky, before another serious attack occurred. While waiting there for James to improve, they heard about Dr. Ephraim McDowell who lived in the nearby village of Danville. McDowell had trained at Scotland's University of Edinburgh as a surgeon, and he specialized in abdominal problems. James's uncle decided they should visit him before going on to Philadelphia. McDowell's examination revealed that James had a urinary bladder stone.[7] The doctor insisted that surgery was the lad's only chance for survival.

James rested for a few days in Danville. Then, on September 12, 1812, the surgeon strapped him tightly to a flat wooden board to hold him down during the delicate operation. McDowell's instruments were crude and unsterilized, and he had nothing except whiskey to ease the patient's blinding pain.

Dr. McDowell watched James carefully to detect any postsurgical complications. The boy's rapid improvement amazed everyone, and he and his uncle went home to Columbia within a few weeks. His pain gradually decreased, and he recovered fully after a year.

By then Samuel Polk had realized that his oldest son was not suited to farmwork. Hoping James might like business better, Samuel arranged a job for him with the owner of a general store in Columbia. However, James hated the work and quit within a few weeks.

All James really wanted was to have a proper education, so his parents enrolled him in the local Zion Church Academy Day School, operated by Reverend Doctor Henderson.[8] James was seventeen, but he did not mind being older than the other students. He lived with a family in a country house nearby, where he took care of his room, cut his firewood, carried his water, and studied the rest of the time.

After an outstanding school year, James transferred to the Bradley Academy in Murfreesboro, Tennessee, run by Samuel P. Black. There he found the same rewards studying Latin and the classics that other students gained from sports and physical activity. James's confidence blossomed as he learned to set goals and achieve them. He came to understand that success depended on discipline, determination, and hard work. The intense studies, coupled with his mother's Calvinist teachings, kept him from wasting a minute.

In January 1816, at the age of twenty, James entered the University of North Carolina as a second-year student. His academic talents and leadership skills greatly increased his self-image. An excellent debater, James was elected president of the Dialectic Society, one of two debate clubs on campus.[9] One of his essays on American liberty won a prize. The shy, reserved young man also made good friends among the university's eighty students.

In June 1818, James earned his degree with highest honors in mathematics and the classics. He believed these subjects would give his mind the most discipline.[10] James's choice was confirmed when he was chosen to deliver the welcoming address in Latin. After graduation he was so tired that he had to rest for four months before going home to Columbia in October.

Following a visit with his family, James went to Nashville to read law with Felix Grundy. A former congressman and a self-educated man, Grundy was Tennessee's most important criminal attorney. He had never lost a capital murder case.[11] James studied hard through 1819 and passed the Tennessee Bar exam in 1820. He opened his own law office in Columbia, where he promptly took on several clients as well as all his family's legal matters.

When the position of clerk of the Tennessee state

Polk's parents built this home in Columbia, Tennessee, while James was at the University of North Carolina. Today, the house is part of the Polk Memorial Association.

senate came open, James asked Grundy to help him obtain it. Polk was appointed in late 1820 and held the post for two years. His job was to direct the flow of paperwork concerning laws, votes, amendments, and other business. He kept track of which senators spoke, their subjects, and what decisions were made. He earned six dollars a day for the few weeks each year the senate was in session, and he practiced law in Columbia between meetings.

After two years as senate clerk, Polk knew his true passion was politics, not the law. Knowing Grundy had given him powerful political contacts. Through Grundy,

Polk met many influential men, including Tennessee's heroic military general, Andrew Jackson.

In 1823, Polk decided to run for elective office. He had two reasons for doing so. The first was his great interest in the Democratic party. The second involved his personal life: Polk was thinking of getting married.

Sarah, the young lady he had in mind, was born to Elizabeth and Joel Childress of Murfreesboro, Tennessee, on September 4, 1803. Sarah's father, a wealthy landowner, was the leader of the county's Democratic party and a longtime friend of Andrew

The parlor in the Polk family home is maintained today in the decorative style of the Polks' time. Many of their personal possessions were gifts from others, including Andrew Jackson.

Jackson's. Sarah called Jackson "Uncle Andrew," and he nicknamed her "Sally." She had learned about politics by listening to her father's conversations with Jackson.

The Childresses had given each of their four children an excellent education. The two girls had a tutor at home who also taught the two boys at Bradley Academy. When Sarah was thirteen, she traveled two hundred miles on horseback with her sister to Salem Female Academy in North Carolina.[12] The school, run by a religious community called the Moravians, attracted bright girls from all over the east. Sarah loved academic subjects and spent her leisure time reading philosophy and Latin. She was bored by the traditional classes for girls in domestic arts, piano, and needlepoint.

James and Sarah had both studied with Reverend Black years earlier, when he was nineteen and she was twelve. When they met again in 1823, James was twenty-eight and considering his future. He decided to ask Andrew Jackson for advice.

Jackson knew James was popular with the ladies of Murfreesboro, and he grumbled, "Stop your philandering! You must settle down as a sober married man!"

Polk was stunned into silence. Finally, he asked, "Which lady shall I choose?"

Jackson replied, "The one who will never give you any trouble! Her wealth, family, education, health, and appearance are all superior. You know her well."

"You mean Sarah Childress?" Polk asked? After a pause, he said, "I shall go at once and ask her."[13]

This official White House portrait of Sarah Childress Polk was painted in 1846 by George Peter Alexander Healy.

Sarah teased Polk, promising to marry him if he won a seat in the Tennessee legislature, so he promptly entered the race. He rode across Maury County for months, speaking to individuals, groups, and those who were too busy to come to political meetings. His hard work and family connections helped him win easily.

Sarah and James were married on January 1, 1824, in a big, lively country wedding at her family's plantation. He later joked that she might not have married him if he had remained a clerk of the senate.[14]

Polk spent his term in the state legislature as chief lieutenant for Governor William Carroll. Among his fellow representatives were Davy Crockett, the frontiersman from the western district, and Felix Grundy of Nashville.

In the legislature, Grundy and Polk remained friends, although they often found themselves on opposite sides of a political question. In one debate, the older man sensed that his former student was about to make a very significant point. Grundy commented aloud to the legislators, "I believe . . . that I have been preparing a club here with which my own head is about to be broken."[15]

3

THE CONGRESSMAN

The Polks' first home in Columbia was a two-room log house. Sarah found it the perfect size because it did not require much housekeeping. She had plenty of time to help her husband in August 1825 when he ran for Tennessee's sixth district seat in the United States House of Representatives.

Polk recognized his limitations as a campaigner. His personality was not naturally lighthearted or outgoing, and he had far more education than most voters in his area. He worked to bridge the gaps by creating a "new" Polk out of his gritty determination to win. He spoke to the voters in simple, direct language. He pleased the crowds with amusing stories and quick retorts. Polk's efforts were rewarded, and he won the election.

Sarah Polk stayed home when her husband left in

October for Washington City, as the nation's capital was called then. He traveled with other members of the Tennessee delegation on horseback over the mountains and along the National Road to Baltimore, Maryland.[1] They boarded the horses in a stable near town to await their return the following March. Then they took a stagecoach the last forty miles and arrived well before the congressional session began.

Polk entered Congress in the fall of 1825, during the administration of President John Quincy Adams. Polk deeply resented the way in which Adams had defeated his good friend Andrew Jackson in the 1824 presidential election: Neither man had received a majority of the popular vote, and the Constitution required that the House of Representatives choose a winner. Henry Clay of Kentucky, a longtime Jackson rival, was Speaker of the House at the time. Rumors buzzed that Clay had persuaded Kentucky's delegates to vote for Adams, even though the Kentucky state legislature expected its delegates to support Jackson. Whether or not such whispers were true, the House elected Adams.

The new president promptly made a serious political mistake. He filled his first and most important Cabinet position by naming Henry Clay as his secretary of state. Jackson supporters accused Adams and Clay of conspiracy, or plotting together. The public was furious. Clay's appointment was called a "corrupt bargain," a payoff in exchange for Kentucky's votes.[2] The scandal hurt Adams's presidency and haunted Clay's career for years.

Polk's first congressional speech came in March 1826. His friendship with Jackson made him the logical man to propose an amendment to the Constitution. If this amendment were to pass, it would require that future presidents be elected by popular vote. The House of Representatives would no longer be the deciding voice in the outcome of close elections.

As expected, the amendment did not pass. However, the speech brought Polk some notable recognition. In it, he stressed that the president was the chief executive of the entire nation and the only federal officer elected by all the people.[3] Polk said the office of president ranked above all other considerations.

In late 1826, Polk persuaded Sarah to go with him to Washington for the second half of his term. When she suggested that it might be more practical for her to stay home again to take care of the house, he insisted, "Why? If it burns down, we can live without it."[4]

It cost a great deal to live in Washington, and congressmen spent much of their modest salaries on travel and living expenses. The Polks, like many others, lived in a boardinghouse during the few months the House was in session. Most members returned to their regular jobs for the rest of the year, as did Polk with his law practice in Columbia.[5]

Repairs to the Capitol were still incomplete fifteen years after the British had burned the building during the War of 1812. The front columns needed replacement, and there were no stairs to the main floor.[6]

Office space was scarce, especially for new congressmen. Many of them conducted business in their boardinghouses, which provided private bed and sitting rooms. Lodgers took their meals in the common dining room. The Polks often talked politics with congressmen who lived nearby, like Franklin Pierce of New Hampshire and John C. Calhoun of South Carolina. Pierce once said he liked to discuss politics with Sarah Polk more than with most men.[7]

Sarah was not a typical congressional wife. She expressed her thoughts openly, often to the amusement of her husband. She visited the ladies' gallery in the House almost daily, staying longer and hearing more than 90 percent of the members.[8]

In August 1827, Polk won his second term in the House. He was appointed to the Committee on Foreign Affairs two months later.[9] His delight was overshadowed in November by the death of his father, Samuel, who passed to him the leadership of the Polk clan. James and Sarah assumed responsibility for their extended family, which included his mother, Jane, who still lived in Columbia.

In the summer of 1828, Polk campaigned for Andrew Jackson's second presidential race. He crossed Tennessee on horseback, trying to reach every voter. He vouched for Jackson as a loyal, generous, considerate, sensitive man. Polk knew his friend could also be feisty and quick-tempered.

Other important facts about the candidate were less

well known. Jackson was a lawyer and former justice of the Tennessee Superior Court. He had made a fortune as a planter and land speculator and married into Nashville's wealthy Donelson family. A great military hero in the War of 1812, Jackson had served in both houses of Congress. However, he had resigned from the Senate five months into his first term, due to boredom.[10]

The "candidate of the people" won the presidency in November 1828 by a huge margin of one hundred forty thousand popular votes. He also took two thirds of the electoral college votes.[11] Polk arranged every detail of Jackson's victory trip from Nashville, Tennessee, to Washington, D. C.[12] Big, boisterous crowds jammed Pennsylvania Avenue from the Capitol to the White House as they celebrated the triumph of the man they affectionately called "Old Hickory."

Once in office, Jackson went straight to business. His opinion on internal improvements was tested early in his term. In 1830, Kentucky requested federal money to build the Maysville Road, a highway completely within the state's borders. Polk and Jackson opposed the road because it would be used only by Kentucky residents. The two men believed that each state should pay for its own internal improvements and that federal funds should be used for projects that would benefit the entire nation. Polk led the opposition to the Maysville Road in the House, and President Jackson vetoed the bill proposing its construction.

In 1831, the Polks suffered several personal

America's seventh president, Andrew Jackson, was painted in oils by Thomas Sully. Jackson was Polk's great friend and political mentor.

tragedies. James's brother Frank died of complications stemming from alcoholism at the age of twenty-eight. Soon after that, James also lost his brothers Marshall and John, both in their middle twenties, who died within a few months of each other.[13] James and Sarah were heartbroken because the family meant so much to them. The Polks had no children of their own, perhaps as a result of the surgery in his teens.

The couple poured their energies into politics. James worked hard in Congress, and Sarah managed their business and social engagements. She was a warm, charming hostess who developed a wide circle of influential friends for her husband. She was at ease in most situations and comfortable discussing many subjects, unlike her husband who was more reserved. James had not come from a background that emphasized social graces. Sarah's lively conversation and gracious attention to her guests were a great help to his career.

Polk took on increasing responsibilities in the House throughout the 1830s. He was appointed to the powerful House Ways and Means Committee, which controlled the raising of federal revenues, including taxes and tariffs. As a committee member, Polk worked closely with the president to solve a major financial crisis in the summer of 1832. It developed shortly before Jackson's race for a second presidential term against Whig candidate Henry Clay.

Jackson needed to settle the issue regarding the Bank of the United States. He believed Congress had created the bank without proper constitutional authority. He also suspected the bank and its president, Nicholas Biddle, of favoring big businesses and eastern manufacturers over the needs of working people.

The bank's business charter was due to expire in 1836. Biddle was planning to renew the charter at that time. However, Henry Clay persuaded him to apply for renewal in 1832, four years early. Clay wanted the bank to become a big enough issue in the coming campaign to interfere with Jackson's reelection.

On July 10, 1832, Jackson vetoed the bank's application to renew its charter, as expected. He soon weakened the bank further by withdrawing from it federal deposits valued at $11 million. Polk supported the president's decision to place these funds in several state banks, known as "pet" banks.[14] Despite his battle with the bank, Jackson won reelection easily.

In December 1833, Polk became chairman of the House Ways and Means Committee. Within weeks he earned national recognition by making a speech in the House supporting Jackson's position on the bank. Polk declared that the Bank of the United States had been so poorly managed and controlled that the president had no choice but to withdraw the government's money.[15]

Next, Jackson turned his attention to import tariffs, or taxes. Imports were products made in other countries and sold in America. Tariffs were taxes that the United States government added to the price of imported goods to make them more expensive than similar items made in the United States. The idea was that if a foreign product cost more than a similar domestic one, people would be more likely to buy the domestic product. The question for Jackson was how much tariff should be added to an import before it was sold.

Vice-President Martin Van Buren came from New York, an area with many manufacturers. He liked high tariffs because they protected local products from having to compete with less costly imports. Senator John C. Calhoun of South Carolina represented an agricultural region that had few manufacturers. Cheap imports were good for the South's agricultural economy: Because southerners bought many imports, Calhoun wanted low tariffs to keep prices on the imports down.

The issue dragged on for months without a solution. Tariffs were blamed for the stalemate, or tie, but the real power struggle was about the rights of individual states to make decisions independent of the federal government. Senator Henry Clay of Kentucky finally wrote a compromise bill that appeared to satisfy everyone for a while.

Polk ran for Speaker of the House in October 1833, but lost to Whig congressman John Bell by ten votes. The two competed again in December 1835, when Polk received 132 votes to 84 for Bell.[16] He had won the most important position in the House of Representatives.

4

THE TEXAS ISSUE

James Polk had no time to rest when he took up his duties as Speaker of the House of Representatives in 1835. The United States had serious matters that required his immediate attention. One problem was the Texas Territory. Polk had never laid eyes on Texas, although he soon came to know it well.

Americans began to notice the empire of Mexico in 1821, when that country gained its independence from Spain. Posters appeared throughout the South and the Mississippi River valley during the same year. They advertised cheap land for sale in a northern province of Mexico called Texas.

The posters failed to mention that much of Texas was wild and desolate. It was a rough, neglected place, hundreds of miles from the capital in Mexico City. Most

34

of the Indian inhabitants were unfriendly, the climate produced droughts, and diseases were a fact of life.

Stephen Austin's posters announced his intention to open a colony for three hundred American settlers in November 1821, on land the Mexican government had granted to his father the year before. Thousands of people wrote to Austin, asking about the property he called "the Old Three Hundred." His ads described it as ". . . good in every respect as man could wish for, Land all first rate, plenty of timber, fine water—beautifully rolling. . . ."[1]

Many people were eager for adventure, and some of the braver ones left the United States to live in Mexico. During the 1820s, the letters G. T. T. began to appear on buildings across the South. The initials indicated the owners had Gone To Texas.

About two thousand Americans moved to Austin's settlement. Imperial Colonization Law in Mexico required every married settler who planned to raise cattle there to pay the government two hundred dollars. In return each would receive 4,428 acres of land. For crop land, married farmers were required to pay two hundred dollars for 177 acres. The Mexican government expected American settlers to become Mexican citizens and to join the Catholic Church.[2]

Mexico banned slavery when the country became independent from Spain in 1821. The Imperial Colonization Law stated ". . . there shall be neither sale nor purchase of slaves in the empire."[3] However, some

American settlers from the South ignored the law and brought their slaves with them when they moved because there were no reliable sources of labor in the Texas Territory to work the land.

In the fifteen years following its independence, Mexico had several unstable governments led by ten presidents and one emperor. On April 6, 1830, the government then in power ordered that no more Americans could settle in Mexico, and for the first time, the Mexican government levied taxes on the Americans who had already settled there. Old-timers believed these decisions threatened their years of hard work and financial gain.

In 1835, a new constitution was written by Antonio López de Santa Anna, the new Mexican president, a dictator who called himself the "Napoleon of the West." Santa Anna canceled certain rights that American settlers had been given years earlier. To deal with these changes, the Americans began to organize their own provisional government in the winter of 1835–1836.

On February 23, 1836, Santa Anna, wearing the uniform of a general, arrived in San Antonio with more than four thousand soldiers. He was determined to halt the budding independence movement and to rid Texas of the "perfidious foreigners" who came from America.[4]

One hundred eighty-two Texans and a large number of their Mexican friends gathered in the Alamo, a sturdy old Catholic mission named for the cottonwood trees around it. In the group were Jim Bowie, maker of the famed Bowie hunting knife, and frontiersman Davy Crockett, who had been Polk's friend in the Tennessee state legislature. The Texans set up whatever defenses they could and waited.

Meanwhile, during the same week, fifty-five American settlers held a meeting, which they called the Texas Convention, in the community of Washington-on-the-Brazos. On March 2, 1836, the group declared Texas to be an independent country, no longer a province of Mexico.

Santa Anna's troops attacked the Alamo for two weeks. Inside the mission, supplies and ammunition ran low, and no help came. The Mexican Army launched its final assault on March 6. All but a few people in the Alamo died, and Santa Anna suffered a staggering loss of sixteen hundred men. The bodies of the dead Texans were burned in a funeral pyre at the end of the day.

The Texas Convention's declaration of independence had enraged Santa Anna. He pursued his vendetta, or personal war, against the Texans with several more conflicts. After a battle at Goliad on March 19, Santa Anna committed an unpardonable act that violated all known codes of military justice. He ordered the massacre of all American prisoners of war. The cruelty only hardened the Texans' determination to proceed with their independence movement.

On April 21, General Sam Houston and 783 Texas men finally cornered the Mexicans and cut off their retreat. With shouts of "Remember the Alamo!" and

Antonio López de Santa Anna, was president of Mexico and a determined military general.

"Remember Goliad!" the Texans crushed Santa Anna's army to win the Battle of San Jacinto in a mere eighteen minutes.

Santa Anna tried to escape disguised as a peasant, but he was captured the next day. The victorious Texans forced him to sign a treaty that would acknowledge the independence of Texas. However, the Mexican government refused to recognize the document as legitimate, and Santa Anna was removed from power. He left the country soon afterward.

By the summer of 1836, the settler population in Texas numbered nearly thirty thousand Americans, four thousand Mexicans, and five thousand blacks, of which most were slaves. In September, Sam Houston was elected the first president of the Republic of Texas. Voters adopted a constitution, patterned after the American document that established three branches of government. The republic permitted slavery, probably because many settlers were farmers from southern states. Texas then asked the United States to either acknowledge its existence as an independent nation or annex its territory as a state.

The outlined area shows the Republic of Texas from the time it was established in 1836 until it was annexed as part of the United States in March 1845, three days before Polk became president. The republic's territory covered land that eventually became part of six states.

Sam Houston was elected the first president of the Republic of Texas in 1836.

Southerners felt the annexation of Texas would be a great opportunity for economic growth. The South had been expanding its cotton fields and shipping raw fiber to Europe and Great Britain for years. Newer, faster looms were helping meet the growing demand for cloth. Southerners realized the additional cotton fields would require more field hands. This expansion might cause more uprisings, as slaves tried to fight for their freedom. The South blamed such turmoil on northern abolitionists, who were against slavery and wanted to end, or abolish, it. Still, southerners welcomed the prospect of increased lands for their crops, especially if slavery were allowed to continue there.

The North believed that to allow Texas into the Union would encourage the dreadful institution of slavery. Northerners feared that if Texas were annexed, its territory might eventually be divided into four to five southern states. Such a development would change the balance of political power in Congress and create what the North considered a giant "slave power."[5]

Great Britain wanted Texas to be an independent

SOURCE DOCUMENT

ANTI-TEXAS MEETING
AT FANEUIL HALL!

Friends of Freedom!

A proposition has been made, and will soon come up for consideration in the United States Senate, to annex Texas to the Union. This territory has been wrested from Mexico by violence and fraud. Such is the character of the leaders in this enterprise that the country has been aptly termed "that valley of rascals." It is large enough to make *nine* or *ten* States as large as Massachusetts. It was, under Mexico, a free territory. The freebooters have made it a slave territory. The design is to annex it, with its load of infamy and oppression, to the Union. The immediate result may be a war with Mexico—the ultimate result *will be* some 18 or 20 more slaveholders in the Senate of the United States, a still larger number in the House of Representatives, and the balance of power in the hands of the South! And if, when in a minority in Congress, slaveholders browbeat the North, demand the passage of gag laws, trample on the Right of Petition, and threaten, in defiance of the General Government, to hang every man, caught at the South, who dares to speak against their "domestic institutions," what limits shall be set to their intolerant demands and high handed usurpations, when they are in the majority?

All opposed to this scheme, of whatever sect or party, are invited to attend the meeting at the Old Cradle of Liberty, to-morrow, (Thursday Jan. 25,) at 10 o'clock, A. M., at which time addresses are expected from several able speakers.

Bostonians! Friends of Freedom!! Let your voices be heard in loud remonstrance against this scheme, fraught with such ruin to yourselves and such infamy to your country.

January 24, 1838.

Many northern abolitionists used posters like this one from Boston to denounce slavery and to protest statehood for the Texas Territory.

country. If it were, the United States would then be sandwiched between two British allies, with the Oregon Territory to the north and Texas to the south. Americans considered this prospect a threat to their independence, so hard-won from the British just sixty years earlier in the Revolutionary War.

Great Britain maintained strong ties with both Mexico and Oregon. British banks influenced events in Mexico by making loans for great sums of money. Great Britain's goal was to gain access to the Pacific coast, with its large deepwater harbors in Los Angeles, Monterey, San Francisco, and Seattle. All these harbors afforded direct passages to Asia, with which Great Britain had a rich history of trade.

James Polk was a practical man, and as Speaker of the House, he understood that the presence of the Republic of Texas would affect most Americans. In theory, he supported annexation for the security of both the United States and Texas, but he felt the time was not right for such a move.

Meanwhile, many other difficult situations were demanding his attention. Dissatisfied Whigs and other opponents were making his life miserable in many ways. One of Polk's most annoying problems as Speaker of the House was the "Gag Rule." He had no control over this unwritten policy, which had been established to keep antislavery congressmen from the North from discussing slavery in the House. These northern abolitionists had been sending so many petitions to

This engraving shows James K. Polk as Speaker of the House of Representatives. Polk served in Congress for fourteen years, the last four as Speaker.

Congress urging that slavery be ended that these petitions were taking up all of Congress's time. They were preventing the House from tackling the real issues of slavery. Both antislavery and proslavery representatives blamed Polk for their frustrations and for not taking their side in the argument.

Polk kept his thoughts on slavery to himself as he weathered the congressional storms. His private views were in conflict. As a southerner whose family had owned plantations for generations, he understood the economic importance of slave labor. On the other hand, as an educated lawyer and a fair man, he also understood the brutal injustice of the system. He was extremely concerned about the growing gap between the North and South on the matter.

In 1836, the nation's money supply spiraled out of control. Polk worked with President Jackson during this government crisis. State banks were issuing credit and paper money, or government bank notes, more freely than had the Bank of the United States. Finally, the economy was crumbling under the burden of too many people taking out too many loans they were unable to pay back to buy things they did not need.

Jackson tried to stop the runaway financial crisis with a document called the Specie Circular. It required that property be purchased only with gold or silver, not with paper money. Land speculation and loans on credit stopped almost overnight. Financial organizations began to fail, bringing on an economic crash called the Panic of 1837.

The Panic began soon after Jackson's presidency had ended and he had retired to his estate in Kentucky. The new president, Democrat Martin Van Buren, took office in March 1837. Within two months, Van Buren and the country were trapped in a serious economic depression.

Thousands of Americans lost their homes and financial security as the crisis worsened. Hundreds of businesses failed and jobs disappeared. Some industrial cities looked like ghost towns. People who lost everything in the Panic became part of a national migration seeking better luck almost anywhere else. The collapse was to last for several years.

By August 1838, James Polk was exhausted and in need of a change. On August 30, he announced that he planned to run for governor of Tennessee. Jackson had encouraged him to run because the Democrats needed Polk's political strength to block the growing Whig power in his home state.

In August 1839, Polk defeated Whig governor Newton Cannon by a narrow margin of 2,462 votes.[6] Once in office, Polk tried to reorganize Tennessee's state banks, but the Whigs fought him at every turn. Polk's efforts ended in failure. He largely avoided Nashville's social scene, claiming he had too much work to do. This solitary attitude did not help his sagging popularity.

Voters were angry with Polk in 1840 because he supported President Van Buren's reelection campaign.

They still blamed Van Buren for all the trouble that followed the Panic of 1837. Van Buren was defeated, and Whig candidate William Henry Harrison was elected president with John Tyler as his vice-president.

In 1841, Polk paid dearly for having supported Van Buren. Tennessee voters turned against him and elected James C. Jones their governor. James Polk was without a job for the first time in his adult life. He faced Jones a second time in 1843, and Jones won again.

A man rarely given to brooding, Polk called the second loss to Jones "the darkest hour of my political life."[7] He and Sarah went home to Columbia, where he resumed his law practice. James Knox Polk firmly believed his best days had come and gone and that his public life was over.

5

THE DARK HORSE

Baltimore was hot on May 27, 1844. The mood inside Odd Fellows Hall was even hotter. There, 266 delegates to the Democratic convention were gathered to select a presidential candidate for the November election. They knew Henry Clay had been chosen as the Whig party candidate a month earlier.

Throughout the spring, most Democrats had expected the favorite, former president Martin Van Buren, to win nomination easily. Although he had lost his bid for a second term in 1840, many considered him the party's most able and experienced leader. They believed that, barring trouble, 1844 would be Van Buren's year for a political comeback.

However, trouble did find Van Buren. He became involved in events concerning Texas. On April 12, 1844,

President John Tyler announced he had signed a treaty with representatives of Texas to annex the republic to the United States. Tyler quickly sent the document to the Senate for ratification, or approval.

People were stunned. Responses came quickly. On April 27, only one month before the Democrats gathered for their convention, two newspapers published comments severely criticizing Tyler's action. The pro-Whig paper, the *National Intelligencer*, printed a letter from Henry Clay stating his strong opposition to annexation.

The pro-Democrat Washington paper, *The Globe*, printed a letter from Martin Van Buren. The former president wrote that although he might favor annexation eventually, right now he considered it best to wait until Mexico was prepared to accept Texas as part of the United States.[1] Van Buren was trying to stay neutral in an effort to keep the Democrats united and save his chance for nomination.

Southern Democrats, who strongly favored annexation, were furious with Van Buren. They demanded an end to all support for him. Rumors indicated that the party had to nominate a strongly pro-annexation candidate. If they did not, some Democratic southerners would break away from the party and hold their own convention. Senator John C. Calhoun of South Carolina, a fiery and outspoken supporter of slavery and annexing Texas, was their most likely candidate. Yet Calhoun's nomination could divide the Democratic party beyond repair.

The Democrats were in turmoil, and former president Andrew Jackson knew he must do something. He was still the party's most influential statesman, even though he lived far from Washington's political spotlight. Jackson was the voice for those who believed America should continue to settle new lands in the west. When he spoke, people listened.

Jackson summoned Polk to Kentucky and told him that Van Buren's letter to *The Globe* had been a serious mistake that could destroy the man's chance for reelection. Jackson believed his party's win in November depended on uniting the Democrats behind a candidate from the southwest who strongly favored annexation. Jackson told Polk he was the only one who filled all the requirements for "the most available man."[2]

Polk was taken aback. He realized some people considered him a vice-presidential possibility, but backing from someone as important as Jackson surprised him. Polk wrote later to his friend, Cave Johnson, "I have never aspired so high."[3] Polk thought it over for a few days and decided Jackson was right. Polk would be ready if Martin Van Buren failed to win the nomination.

Senator Robert J. Walker of Mississippi worked behind the scenes in the weeks before the Democratic convention. Walker had written a newspaper article early in the year called a "Letter . . . Relative to the Annexation of Texas." His piece discussed the great economic gains the nation would receive from annexation, and the certainty he felt that all the people would benefit.

Walker also mentioned the sensitive problem of racial prejudice in every state. He believed that expanding the country offered the South's large population of surplus slaves new places to live and work. With the annexation of Texas, they could go to Mexico, where slavery had been banned since 1821.

Senator Walker was ready when the Democratic convention opened on May 27. His anger over Van Buren's failure to take a stand on Texas in his letter drove Walker to make sure the man from New York would not be nominated. Walker convinced the convention delegates to select a chairman who disliked both Van Buren and his supporters.

Walker's next step was for his allies to propose a change in the method of voting for candidates. The new rule would require a two-thirds majority, or 177 votes, to win the nomination. Previous winners needed only a simple majority equal to half the votes, plus one.

Walker's people pushed for the voting change despite loud shouts of protest throughout Odd Fellows Hall. Many delegates had come to the convention already pledged to a specific candidate for the first ballot. After that, they would be free to vote for whomever they wished.

The New Yorkers knew Van Buren had enough votes to win a simple majority on the first ballot. However, his position would be less secure if the convention were to adopt the proposed two-thirds requirement.

The delegates discussed the rule change for two days. Benjamin Butler, head of the New York delegation, battled the plan. Senator Walker stayed on the sidelines to relish the spectacle he had created. When the group finally voted, the proposal to require a two-thirds majority passed by a good margin. The outcome even included some "yea" votes from Van Buren delegates.

The men then began to vote for candidates. Van Buren received a simple majority on the first ballot, but he fell short of a two-thirds vote. By the fourth round, he could see a second presidential term slipping away. Senator Lewis Cass of Michigan, an outspoken supporter of expansion, won an increasing number of votes as Van Buren's totals declined.

The candidates' supporters and detractors met privately behind closed doors. They cornered each other in the hallways to discuss new strategies. By the fifth ballot, Cass was the front-runner, and Van Buren's team was losing heart for the race. After the seventh ballot, the exhausted delegates adjourned for the night.

However, the party leadership did not rest. These men talked long past midnight, revising plans and proposing alternative deals. The voting deadlock hurt not only the candidates, but the convention and the party as well. The Van Buren and Cass factions disliked each other so much that a radical new plan was needed that would be acceptable to both sides.

George Bancroft, leader of the Massachusetts delegation and a renowned historian, offered a possible solution to the impasse. Though a Van Buren supporter himself, Bancroft suggested James Knox Polk of Tennessee.[4] Polk had not been on the first seven ballots. He had not received a single write-in vote. Bancroft believed Polk was the ideal compromise candidate.

Bancroft reviewed Polk's experience for the delegates. James Polk had spent fourteen consecutive years in Congress, including four as Speaker of the House. He was a former governor of Tennessee, and a southwesterner who strongly favored expansion. He was a close friend of Andrew Jackson's in whom the public still had great confidence. Polk had good relationships with most Democrats. In addition, some believed they owed him something for trying to keep the governorship of Tennessee in the party.

George Bancroft, Robert J. Walker, and Polk's manager, Gideon Pillow, worked through the night of May 28, persuading delegates that Polk was the right choice. New Hampshire and Massachusetts finally decided to go with him, as did Alabama and Mississippi.[5]

On the morning of May 29, the delegates were polled for the eighth ballot. Cass still led, Van Buren was second, and Polk came in third with forty-four votes.[6] No one received a two-thirds majority. Excitement built as delegates began to see a way out of their dilemma. They had found a candidate who could satisfy most factions without offending anyone.

The convention chairman called for the ninth ballot. The first delegation declared immediately for James Polk. The next state followed suit. Momentum grew and the rush was on. The delegates from New York, home of Martin Van Buren, were gracious in defeat as their leader announced the state's votes for Polk.

Whoops and laughter resounded in Odd Fellows Hall as state after state clamored to add their votes to the tally. The atmosphere was electric as last holdouts among Cass delegates switched their votes. Finally, the Democrats proclaimed James Knox Polk their candidate for president.

"I never saw such enthusiasm, such *exultation,* such *shouting for joy,*" Gideon Pillow bellowed above the din.[7] Polk was the first Democratic nominee ever chosen because of a deadlock in the voting. From then on, he was known as the first "dark horse" presidential candidate. The term was racing jargon, used to indicate a relatively unknown competitor who came from behind to win a race. It described Polk perfectly. Surely the Democratic nominee was an unexpected victor, and he had loved horses all his life.

After lengthy celebrations, the delegates began to choose a vice-presidential candidate. There was a bit of drama when Silas Wright of New York, the first choice, declined the nomination by telegraph. Wright felt the convention had been unfair to his friend, Van Buren.

George Mifflin Dallas of Boston was the second choice for vice-president, and he won nomination easily.

He was a lawyer with a good business background, particularly in imports and tariffs. He brought a moderate northern viewpoint to the ticket as a balance to Polk's southern roots. Dallas was married to Senator Walker's niece, and the couple had strong political connections.

The delegates' last task was to adopt a campaign platform that represented the party's opinions, known as planks, on important issues. The platform included the usual Democratic principles favoring smaller government and lower taxes and tariffs.

The platform contained two new planks in 1844. The first was that all of the Oregon Territory rightfully belonged to the United States; and the second was that the party intended to pursue the acquisition of both Oregon and Texas.[8]

The telegraph line between Baltimore and Washington flashed the news of the nomination. James and Sarah Polk were waiting at home in Columbia, Tennessee. He replied at once, accepting the delegates' invitation, but with one highly unusual stipulation: James Knox Polk stated that if elected, he would serve only one term. Then he would return to private life.

6

THE ROAD TO THE WHITE HOUSE

Who is James K. Polk?" Whigs encouraged crowds to shout this singsong slogan whenever Polk's name was mentioned during the campaign of 1844.[1] They considered the Democratic candidate to be incredibly dull and largely unknown outside Washington.

The experiences and personal styles of the two major candidates gave voters a distinct choice. The Whigs believed there was no comparison between Polk and their candidate, Henry Clay. Clay was better known, a point he seldom failed to mention, while Polk was the dark horse. The Democrats ignored the insults and focused on campaign issues. They did not regard Polk's serious personality as a drawback.

Clay frequently favored both sides of an issue at

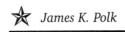

Henry Clay of Kentucky, Polk's opponent in the presidential election of 1844, was a prominent figure in the Whig party. He had been secretary of state for the sixth president, John Quincy Adams.

different times or reversed his position whenever he wished. That happened when he published a letter in April 1844 opposing the annexation of Texas and later changed his mind. Clay's opponents called his strategy "weaseling," or "talking out of both sides of his mouth."[2] Although Clay confused the public at times, his personal charm usually saved him from criticism.

The Democrats were the party of Andrew Jackson and the common man. The Whig party had been forged twenty years earlier from several groups who opposed Jackson. By 1844, the Whigs finally offered a platform of solid issues, including higher taxes, a regulated currency, and a single-term presidency.

Polk's nomination came at an exciting time for America. The country was growing in all directions. Polk shared the views of expansionists who realized the United States was on the move, free of the last demoralizing traces of the Panic of 1837, and full of enthusiasm about the future.

Americans loved the concept of Manifest Destiny, which was first published in *The United States Magazine and Democratic Review*.[3] It was made popular by John L. O'Sullivan, a thirty-two-year-old editor with the New York *Morning News*.[4]

The concept of Manifest Destiny meant different things to different people. Most thought its interpretation meant God's Will gave them the right to stretch the nation's borders from the Atlantic to the Pacific oceans. The phrase made Americans feel important. National confidence soared. *The New York Herald* said, "A spirit has taken wing from the land of freedom. . . ."[5]

Such energy was fed by rapid growth. In the seven decades between the American Revolution and Polk's election, the number of states increased from thirteen to twenty-seven. During the months of Polk's campaign another new wave of immigrants, primarily Catholics from Ireland and Germany, was settling in America.

Most longtime citizens were Protestants and Whig party members. Many disliked Catholics and resented their arrival in this country. In contrast, Democrats warmly welcomed all new arrivals. In return, their party often received support from appreciative newcomers at election time.

Before 1800, people had begun to carve paths through the forests on their way to the western frontier. Between 1804 and 1806, Meriwether Lewis and William Clark fueled America's interest when President Jefferson sent them in search of the Northwest Passage. They did not find it, although they explored as far west as the Pacific Ocean.

Within a few years, a new breed of adventurers called mountain men followed in their footsteps. The loners, with memorable names like Jedediah Smith, Zebulon Pike, and Kit Carson, explored throughout the Rocky Mountains, California, and Oregon. Each went his solitary way for months, collecting fur pelts to sell or trade. Sometimes they came to the annual trappers' gathering held along the Green River in the Oregon

Territory.[6] The Green River site was an important landmark for settlers headed for Oregon. When they reached this site these adventurous pioneers felt a sense of triumph over the mountain ranges, deserts, wild animals, hostile natives, severe weather, and natural disasters they had tackled along the way.

America's wide-open spaces brought new challenges as well as benefits. Sometimes, farmers who relocated far from major waterways had trouble moving their crops to market before they spoiled. Help came in 1825, when New York State built the Erie Canal, connecting the Great Lakes with the Atlantic Ocean. The link allowed crops, raw materials, and manufactured products to be shipped quickly and safely. In addition, steam-driven, paddle-wheel boats were developed for the shallower inland rivers. These paddle-wheelers ferried families, businessmen, cargo, and gamblers together on the same trip.

Meanwhile, the east was not idle. Cities like Boston and Philadelphia became centers of wealth and political power. England's Industrial Revolution provided a

Steam-driven paddle-wheel boats, like the one in the center of the picture, carried cargo and passengers to inland towns and cities.

stream of new technology that changed the way Americans did business.

Inventors developed machines to replace work formerly done by hand. Government patents for inventions tripled during the 1840s.[7] Companies built factories and hired more workers to operate the new equipment. Farmers flocked to cities, seeking jobs with higher wages.

Commercial activity was brisk all along the Atlantic coast. Seaports in Boston, New York, Philadelphia, and Charleston had natural deepwater harbors. Sailing vessels from around the world docked at their piers to take on cargo.

Early railroads, built in the 1830s, carried passengers and freight over nine thousand miles of newly laid track. By 1844, trains reached toward all corners of the nation. At the same time, telegraph companies strung wires in an ever-widening net across cities and towns, prairies and deserts, and into risky, hard-to-reach outposts.

The election campaign of 1844, like most others, began with both candidates trying to take credit for the country's successes and blaming its problems on the other party. Of course, no one claimed responsibility for workers who labored from dawn to dark, six days a week, in dangerous and unhealthy conditions, for wages that were painfully unfair. No one accepted the blame for failing to provide laws to protect young children from illness, injury, or even death on the job.

In August 1844, the pro-Democratic New York

newspapers began to call Polk "Young Hickory." The term was an obvious compliment that referred to his close friendship with Andrew Jackson, commonly known as "Old Hickory." Jackson's troops in the Tennessee state militia had given him the nickname many years earlier, and it had stuck.

The Polks remained at home in Columbia throughout most of the campaign. Sarah served as her husband's personal secretary, confidante, and organizer of campaign activities. She read many newspapers every day, clipping articles he should read, and putting them on a chair outside his office.[8] She also wrote some of his letters and received many visitors each day.

Polk exchanged letters with key supporters in every state. He depended on them to explain his opinions to the voters. Everyone was interested in the Texas and Oregon territories. Businessmen cared about tariffs and setting up an independent treasury free of government meddling and party politics. Polk wanted his opinions on these issues to be repeated at every opportunity.

Every state belonged to the Electoral College. Each was allotted a number of electoral votes based on the size of its population. Smaller states had fewer votes, and larger ones had more.

James Birney, the Liberty party candidate, lived in New York State. His small party was interested only in antislavery causes. Birney did not draw many votes across the nation, but he received enough in his home state to affect the election results.

Votes were counted during several November days in cities, towns, villages, farms, and along the frontier. Polk won the election with a small margin of about thirty-eight thousand votes out of nearly 2.7 million that were cast. He took enough states to win 170 Electoral College votes, while Henry Clay gathered only 105.[9]

James Birney received around sixty-two thousand votes nationwide, and sixteen thousand in New York State. Birney's votes came from people who would otherwise have supported Clay if it had been only a two-man race. By pulling votes away from Clay, Birney helped Polk win in New York by about five thousand popular votes. Therefore, Polk received the state's thirty-six electoral votes.[10] In effect, Birney kept Henry Clay from becoming president.

If James Polk had been a card player, poker surely would have been his game. He knew the outcome of the election before news began to spread, but he did not say a word.

The mail train from New York had arrived in Nashville, Tennessee, at about 9:00 P.M. It carried a scribbled message from the postmaster in Cincinnati, Ohio, who had heard the election results, then quickly penciled a hasty note on the outside of the mail pouch to convey the news to other postmasters down the line. The Nashville postmaster, General Robert Armstrong, saw the message on the pouch. He was a good friend of the Polks, and he quickly sent a messenger to their house with the news.[11]

Polk read Armstrong's note early in the morning, and he said nothing for twenty-four hours. He worked in his office, stopping only to accept condolences from unhappy friends who were assuming the worst as time went by without any news. Polk enjoyed his little jest for a whole day before revealing his great secret.

7

THE OREGON TERRITORY

A month after James Polk took office, he revealed his true intentions to only one man, his secretary of the Navy. George Bancroft was amazed to hear the usually reserved president describe his plans so openly. Bancroft clearly recalled the conversation some forty years later and mentioned it in his memoirs:

> . . . speaking energetically, he [Polk] raised his hand high in the air and bringing it down with force on his thigh, he said, there are to be four great measures of my administration,—
>
> The settlement of the Oregon question with Great Britain.
>
> The acquisition of California and a large district on the coast.

64

The reduction of the Tariff to a revenue basis.

The complete and permanent establishment of the Constitutional Treasury, as he [Polk] loved to call it, but as others had called it, "Independent Treasury. . . ."[1]

In the summer of 1845, a few months after his inauguration, President Polk decided to start keeping a diary. A meeting with Secretary of State James Buchanan inspired him to write down an account of the events that would occur during his term.[2]

His frequent entries revealed the mind of a keen observer and an organized planner. He referred to himself as "the president" at first, but soon changed to "I" or "me." He included everyone's title or military rank and rarely mentioned first names. He even called his wife "Mrs. Polk."

Polk expressed his observations and opinions candidly. He noted things he would not have mentioned in person. The detailed comments took a lot of time, and he wrote whenever he could. Many entries began with the words "after night," meaning after dark. He named senators, Cabinet members, and others who came to the White House on government business, sometimes as late as 10:00 P.M.

The president made his first entry on August 26, 1845, and it was about the Oregon Territory. In the diary, he wrote of his plan to relocate the region's northern border from 42° north latitude, its current position, to 54°40′ north latitude, far up in Canada. The Democrats had widely promoted the idea of increasing

This portrait of Polk was made by H.W. Smith in 1846, about the same time the debate was heating up over the Oregon Territory.

the area of the Oregon Territory in their winning campaign slogan, "Fifty-Four Forty or Fight."

Polk also noted that he did not want to continue managing the Oregon Territory jointly with Great Britain. That joint governing authority had been established by a treaty in 1818 and was renewed at the Convention of 1827. British and American citizens lived, worked, and traded together in the region.

The British had been coming to Oregon since the 1780s or earlier and had made extensive and long-standing investments there. The Hudson's Bay Company, a worldwide trading business, had controlled

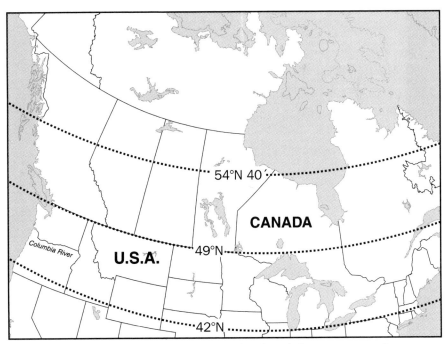

When Polk took office the northern border of the Oregon Territory was at 42°N. Polk wished to increase the territory up to 54°40′N. A compromise position was finally fixed at 49°N.

most of Great Britain's interests in Oregon for twenty years prior to 1845. The company guaranteed fur traders and fishermen plenty of access to major rivers throughout the territory.

In July 1845, Polk's secretary of state, James Buchanan, sent a letter to the British minister in Washington, D.C., Sir Richard Pakenham. Buchanan proposed a compromise plan. He offered to establish the Oregon border at 49° north latitude, instead of at the 54°40´ north latitude. This compromise would place the border at the same latitude as the rest of the United States—from the Atlantic Ocean in the east, through the Rocky Mountains in the center, to the Pacific Ocean in the west. Buchanan's offer did not include navigation rights for the British on the Columbia River. Pakenham rejected the proposal immediately without even consulting his government in London.

On August 26, Polk told his Cabinet that he had also written a letter to Great Britain and was prepared to send it. Polk's letter stated that his compromise offer to settle the Oregon border on 49° north latitude was now being withdrawn and that he would not reconsider the matter. The letter also reemphasized America's "manifest" right to all of Oregon up to 54°40´ north latitude, near the southern tip of Alaska.

The president explained to his Cabinet that he had made the offer, so quickly rejected by the British ". . . in language . . . scarcely courteous or respectful . . . ," in the hope of keeping peace between the two countries.[3]

Polk added that he was not sorry about the British minister's negative response and that Pakenham could go and do whatever he pleased.

Buchanan suggested that Polk postpone sending his letter. The president declined. He said he had thought about Oregon more than anything else since taking office. Buchanan feared Polk's hard-line position would lead to war. Polk responded that if war did come, it would not be America's fault. He then dispatched the letter to the British.

A letter from Andrew Jackson, written in May, had bolstered Polk's thinking. In it, Jackson had encouraged the president to resist Great Britain's false claims to Oregon. Jackson predicted the British were merely trying Polk's patience and would not actually go to war over the territory.

Many Americans saw Oregon as a perfect example of Manifest Destiny. The territory had fertile soil, tall pines, and plenty of fish and game. Most of the natives were friendly. Settlers traveled to the northwest along the Oregon Trail in long trains of up to one hundred wagons. The hazardous trip took several months, and pioneers followed experienced guides or took word-of-mouth advice from earlier emigrants.

In October 1845, Polk began writing his first Annual Message to Congress, to be delivered in December. In the message he linked the issue of Oregon with the Monroe Doctrine. This document, written by former president James Monroe in 1823, stated that no

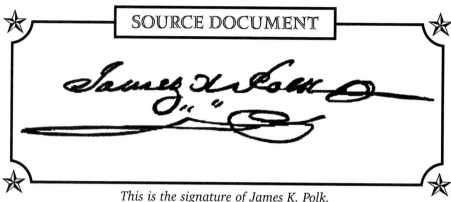

This is the signature of James K. Polk.

European power could plant or establish a new colony on North American soil.

Polk believed the Monroe Doctrine supported his view that Great Britain had no legitimate claim to Oregon. He also revealed he was thinking ahead to a future acquisition of California, as well, when he pointed out that the Monroe Doctrine was specific about the limits of access by foreign governments to ". . . California and the fine bay of San Francisco as much . . . as Oregon."[4]

Missouri senator Thomas Hart Benton often visited Polk to share the latest news about his son-in-law, Lieutenant Colonel John Frémont. The colonel had explored the Rocky Mountains several times with his guide, Kit Carson. Frémont and teams of mapmakers surveyed land for the United States Army.[5]

Polk and Benton often discussed Oregon. The president said it was time to give Great Britain twelve months' notice, as required by the Convention of 1827, to end their joint administration of the territory.

ACCOMPANIMENT TO THE

MAP OF THE EMIGRANT ROAD

FROM INDEPENDENCE, MO.,

T O

ST. FRANCISCO, CALIFORNIA.

B Y

T. H. JEFFERSON.

NEW YORK : published by the author, and for sale by BERFORD & Co.,
2 Astor House. 1849.

Entered according to Act of Congress, in the year 1849, by T. H. JEFFERSON,
in the Clerk's office of the District Court of the Southern District of New York.

BRIEF PRACTICAL ADVICE TO THE EMIGRANT OR TRAVELLER.

THE journey is not entirely a pleasure trip. It is attended with some hardships and privation—nothing, however, but that can be overcome by those of stout heart and good constitution. A small party (10 or 20) of the *proper* persons *properly* outfitted might make a pleasure trip of the journey. Large parties are to be deprecated.

There are two modes of outfit—one with horses, called "packing," the other with wagons, drawn by oxen. The first perform the journey in from 60 to 90 days; the second from four to six months. A walk is the usual gait of all parties. Packing is the safest and most expeditious, and in some respects preferable, even for women and children. Side-saddles should be discarded—women should wear hunting-frocks, loose pantaloons, men's hats and shoes, and ride the same as the men.

The road is a simple wagon trail—part good, and part very bad. Large parties are annoyed by a fine white dust. No dependence can be placed upon game. Take breadstuff enough for the whole journey. Carry nothing but provisions and articles of necessity.

Packers want two horses each ; one to ride, the other to pack. A third to run loose is advisable. Tuckapaw saddle-tree—light pad top

---

The opening page of a pamphlet written for travelers journeying to Oregon and California gives some helpful hints.

The men agreed on the need to build American forts, manned by mounted riflemen, to protect settlers headed for Oregon. The Hudson's Bay Company had already established twenty forts along the Fraser River to guard British citizens. Polk told Benton that the laws of the United States should apply to Americans in the territory. British citizens there had been shielded by the laws of Great Britain since 1821, when Parliament had passed a law to protect them.

At the Cabinet meeting on November 29, Polk and Buchanan disagreed again about where to establish the northern border of Oregon. It was currently located along 42° north latitude. Buchanan still wanted it moved to 49° north latitude. He quoted several congressmen who said Americans would never support a war to increase the territory farther north than that.

Polk disagreed. He said other advisers had insisted on the entire territory, to 54°40′ north latitude. Buchanan's views often annoyed the president. Polk complained in his diary several times that the secretary of state was overly cautious, worried too much, and hesitated to take action. He once wrote that Buchanan ". . . sometimes acts like an old maid."[6]

On December 22, the president received some unexpected support. Former president John Quincy Adams had been reelected to the House of Representatives. Adams notified Polk that although the two had been opponents during Adams's presidency, he approved of

Polk's plans for the Oregon Territory and intended to make his views well known in the House.

A week later, on December 27, Buchanan visited Polk late at night to report that Sir Pakenham was asking for an unnamed friendly power to resolve the Oregon question. The decision was not to be about which country held title, but about how to divide the territory. Polk said no.

Polk's comments about Oregon in his Annual Message to Congress in December 1845 caused a lot of talk. In the message, he revealed that his efforts to compromise had failed and that Congress would have to decide the next move. Some members were afraid that war was coming.

Congressman Black of South Carolina came to warn the president that the Democratic party would split wide open if the United States told Great Britain it wanted to end joint occupation of Oregon. Northwestern senators, who wanted to change the current system, were pitted against southern senators who wanted it to remain the same. Northwesterners were holding out for 54° 40′ north latitude. Senator John C. Calhoun, a southerner, was among those who wanted the border issue to end, almost regardless of the outcome. Black and several senators from central states were looking for a common ground that could satisfy most people. All the factions were at odds, and most people were tired of the subject.

Polk firmly maintained his stand in favor of

informing Great Britain about ending joint occupancy. He told Black, "the only way to treat John Bull [Great Britain] was to look him straight in the eye."[7] Polk believed that if Congress wavered, the British would become even more arrogant and demanding.

In early February 1846, the president heard that some senators wanted to pass a resolution advising him to reopen the Oregon negotiations and settle the matter by compromise. Senator Benton opposed the resolution because it would take decision-making authority out of the president's hands.

On February 10, the House finally passed the resolution to end joint occupancy of Oregon. The Senate discussed the issue in a special session on February 25. Editor Thomas Ritchie of the Washington *Union* newspaper reported that the meeting had been nothing but a loud and angry debate. Calhoun's position in favor of 49° north latitude was adopted, much to the great distress of most northwesterners.

Calhoun came to the White House later the same day. Polk reminded him that a Senate vote required a two-thirds majority for approval. He said the American position would be damaged severely if too few senators voted for 49° north latitude and the measure failed. Sir Pakenham would hear about it within hours and toughen his negotiating position. Polk stood firm that Great Britain had to make the next move. He reminded Calhoun that free navigation for the British on the Columbia River was not open for discussion.

Senator John C. Calhoun from South Carolina sought a compromise on the Oregon Territory border dispute, hoping to promote himself as a peace-loving candidate in the next presidential election.

Polk suspected much of the tension over Oregon was due to the personal goals of some politicians. He believed Calhoun favored a compromise so that voters would see him as the peace candidate. Senators Allen of Ohio and Cass of Michigan refused to compromise, perhaps so they would appear strong in the next presidential election. Senator Benton just wanted a fair solution. Polk wrote on March 4, 1846, "I am left without any certain or reliable support in Congress . . . especially in the Senate. Each leader looks to his own advancement."[8]

Events began to move quickly. At last, on April 27, the president signed a congressional resolution terminating joint administration of Oregon with Great Britain.[9] On June 12, he forwarded Great Britain's most recent compromise proposal to the Senate. Polk wanted its advice because he wished to present a united front when dealing with the British.

On June 15, 1846, the Senate advised Polk to accept Great Britain's offer and finish the matter once and for all. The key elements were (1) 49° north latitude would mark the boundary between the United States and Canada, except for Vancouver Island, which would remain in British hands; and (2) the United States and Great Britain would share free navigation of rivers throughout the territory. These provisions were part of the treaty ratified by the Senate, in a vote of 41 to 14, and forwarded to Polk for signature.[10]

The president was satisfied with the compromise. He

had achieved one of his most important goals without firing a shot. Privately, Polk had believed all along that 49° north latitude was the appropriate and logical boundary for Oregon. He then turned his full attention elsewhere, as war with Mexico had been declared four weeks earlier, on May 13, 1846.

8

THE MEXICAN WAR

Back before Polk was inaugurated, the fate of the Republic of Texas, which had remained independent since 1836, was left unresolved. Sam Houston, the republic's first president, led a government that suffered from serious disorganization and a severe lack of money. European nations, especially Great Britain, kept pressure on Texas not to join the United States.

Americans had their own strong opinions about the republic, and their views hardened over the years. Southerners, who strongly favored annexing Texas, saw it as an opportunity to extend their cotton fields. Northerners, who rejected annexation, believed expansion would merely fuel the growth of slavery and dilute their region's power in Congress.

In 1844, the House and Senate had passed a joint resolution admitting Texas to the Union. Finally, President Tyler signed the document on March 1, 1845, three days before Polk's inauguration, and sent it to the Senate for ratification.

The Mexicans still regarded Texas as part of their own country. They had never really accepted Texas's independence and regarded annexation by the United States as an act of pure aggression. Three weeks after Polk took office, they broke relations with the United States. Mexico ordered its ambassador in Washington to reclaim his passport and return home.

The United States and Mexico disagreed on three important issues: The first was the location of the southwestern border between Texas and Mexico. Mexico wanted the current boundary of the Rio Nueces to remain, but Texas claimed the Rio Grande as its southern border. The second issue was Mexico's refusal to pay American settlers more than $2 million in claims for losses that the Americans had incurred when Mexico changed the settlement rules. The third issue was Mexico's order to remove all Americans from Mexican lands in Alta, or Upper, California.

Regarding the last issue, the United States suspected that Mexico and Great Britain were plotting the eventual occupation of California by the British.[1] Polk kept a wary eye on that possibility.

In mid-June 1845, Polk ordered General Zachary Taylor of the United States Army to advance to "some point on or near" the Rio Grande. On June 24, Polk told Secretary of the Navy George Bancroft to prepare to seize and occupy California ports if war broke out.[2] Bancroft and Commodore John Sloat of the United States Navy began planning to take Monterey, the capital of the Mexican province of Alta California.

In Mexico, two resolutions were passed to expand its army. On July 20, President Jose Herrera asked his Congress to declare war on the United States. He acknowledged the probable loss of Texas, but he wanted to resolve the settlers' financial claims against his government. At the same time, he tried to resume the negotiations, still hoping to avoid an armed conflict with the United States.

By August 1, General Taylor's forces had moved near Corpus Christi at the mouth of the Rio Nueces. They did not go farther south to the Rio Grande, as Polk had directed. Taylor had orders to regard any effort by Mexico to cross the Rio Grande into Texas as "the commencement of hostilities."[3]

Polk mentioned Texas for the first time in his diary on August 29. His interest in the region was both official and personal, because he had relatives in east Texas, near the Louisiana border.

In September, Polk appointed John Slidell as his "Envoy Extraordinary and Minister Plenipotentiary" to Mexico. The wordy title meant Slidell was Polk's diplomatic representative. Polk instructed his diplomat to buy the provinces of Alta California and New Mexico for $20 million. Slidell was also authorized to offer Mexico an additional sum if it would accept the Rio Grande as the southwestern boundary of Texas.

However, the Mexicans declined to receive Slidell when he arrived in Mexico in December. The reason they gave was that they had agreed to negotiate with a middle-level official, not with a high-level diplomat. Mexico also refused to discuss any matter but the border question.

On December 29, 1845, Texas became the twenty-eighth state of the Union. Polk signed the documents twenty years, almost to the day, after he entered Congress to conduct the nation's business.

Two days later, Mexican General Mariano Parades overthrew President Herrera. Parades announced he was prepared to use military force to defend Mexico against the United States, and he ordered ambassador Slidell to go home.

Slidell wrote to the president in mid-January 1846 about his unsuccessful efforts to negotiate the border. Accordingly, Polk ordered Taylor to move southward from the Rio Nueces to the north bank of the Rio Grande. The general relocated his troops six weeks later and camped along the river opposite the fortified town of Matamoros.

On April 12, a Mexican officer warned Taylor to return to the Rio Nueces, and Taylor refused. On April 25, Mexican soldiers crossed the Rio Grande and ambushed an American unit commanded by Captain

The main battle sites of the Mexican War are marked here by cannons.

Seth Thornton. The attackers retreated across the river, leaving sixteen American casualties.

Taylor's report of the clash reached Polk on May 9. The president, who was already considering war with Mexico, reacted quickly. He met with the Cabinet far into the night, and a declaration of war went to the House of Representatives two days later. The vote was 174 for and 14 against it.

The Senate approved the declaration of war the next day, by a vote of forty-two in favor and two opposed, despite strong protests from northern abolitionists. James Knox Walker, Polk's nephew and private secretary, brought news of the bitter debate that had preceded the voting. Senator John C. Calhoun, who was firmly opposed, did not vote.

Unaware that Mexico had attacked again on May 8 and 9, Polk signed the declaration of war on May 13. The United States was now officially at war with Mexico. Although there were several issues, Polk was most concerned with the fates of Texas, California, and New Mexico.

In the afternoon of May 13, Major General Winfield Scott, commanding general of the United States Army, briefed Polk and the Cabinet on his needs for men and equipment to fight the war. The president offered him command of the army to be raised, and Scott accepted. Polk was not certain the general was well suited to the post. However, as the Army's highest ranking officer, Scott was entitled to it.

Meanwhile, Taylor moved into Matamoros on May 18 to wait for the baggage wagons and horses promised by the American government. His army had grown to almost twenty thousand men, and most were volunteers. To supply such a force was a huge task.

Subtropical diseases began to affect Taylor's forces. Malaria and yellow fever caused high fevers, dysentery, and a general loss of strength. The local food and water aggravated the symptoms. Camp conditions were unsanitary, and hundreds of men died. Fortunately, Mexico did not attack during this time.

In July 1846, war reached California in the west. On July 7, Commodore John Sloat occupied the coastal town of Monterey. Commander James B. Montgomery took San Francisco on July 9, and Sloat occupied the city later the same day.

Lieutenant James Revere took the Sacramento Valley town of Sonoma, also on July 9. He raised the American flag on July 11 to end the four-week Bear Flag Revolt, during which Sonoma's settlers had flown a flag carrying the image of a bear to proclaim their independence from Mexico.

Commodore Robert Stockton sailed south toward San Diego on July 12. He occupied several towns along the California coast, including Santa Barbara and Los Angeles. On August 17, Stockton announced that the Mexican province of Alta California had been annexed to the United States.

In midsummer 1846, Americans also annexed the

In this engraving, Commander James B. Montgomery of the United States Navy accepts the surrender of San Francisco in the Mexican province of Alta California on July 9, 1846.

province of New Mexico. In August, Colonel Stephen W. Kearny of the United States Army led his men southwest from Fort Leavenworth in the Kansas Territory. He had orders to occupy the town of Las Vegas, which he did without firing a shot. On August 17, Kearny declared New Mexico part of the United States.

Kearny and his troops were en route to California in September when they encountered the legendary frontier guide and scout Kit Carson as he was returning home to Santa Fe. Carson gave them news about the military successes in California, and then he turned around and led Kearny and his men to the Pacific coast.

In Mexico, on September 19, Taylor's army launched an assault on the well-defended town of Monterrey, Mexico. During the four-day siege, the Americans captured the main road, and then won the battle through vicious, bloody, hand-to-hand fighting. Taylor promptly called an eight-week truce, which displeased Polk and Army headquarters in Washington.

On November 16, Taylor occupied the town of Saltillo. In mid-January 1847, he heard that General Santa Anna had returned to Mexico and was on the march with twenty thousand men. Taylor's army was outnumbered three to one.

Taylor's men took defensive positions and waited in the hacienda, or ranch, at Buena Vista. They suffered heavy losses the first day but rallied the next morning. That day, the tide of battle turned when Colonel Jefferson Davis led a dramatic charge and Captain

Braxton Bragg directed a major assault against the Mexicans. Buena Vista was the final conflict in northern Mexico. Taylor and a small force stayed on until November before returning to the United States. Most of Taylor's army moved south to join Major General Scott in Mexico, where he was planning a march to Mexico City from the coastal town of Vera Cruz.

Polk was not impressed with General Taylor. The president considered him a courageous and self-confident man, but one who did not do his job properly. Polk wrote twice in his diary that Taylor was ". . . wholly incompetent for so large a command."[4] He also noted that Taylor was a hard fighter, but ". . . from the beginning . . . he has been constantly blundering into difficulties . . ." which cost many lives.[5]

The president had an equally low regard for middle-ranking officers. Many were untrained political appointees with weak leadership skills and little dedication. Most were Whigs, and political rivalry clouded their dealings with the Democratic administration.

Though Polk had never served in the military, he was drawn into planning the war. On May 14, 1847, he wrote that the ". . . conduct of the war . . . devolves upon . . . myself a vast amount of labour."[6] This planning cost him valuable time, but Polk could be assured that schedules and requirements were met. The president frequently helped Secretary of War William Marcy, whose health ". . . may be destroyed and his life endangered" from overwork.[7]

War information came to Washington by courier, steamship, or train and was often outdated before it arrived. Polk worried about making plans based on faulty data. The new telegraph carried only limited reports from New Orleans, Louisiana. As a result, wild rumors spread quickly, and the worst ones were repeated endlessly.

Polk used several means to collect good information, including secret agents in Mexico. They were doctors, military officers, newspaper reporters, and others in a position to hear or overhear confidential news and report it directly to Polk.

By early 1847, the brief war in the west had been won. On January 13, Mexican leader Pio Pico surrendered the province of Alta California and signed the Treaty of Cahuenga to end hostilities there.

The campaign in Mexico was still under way. In February 1847, General Scott gathered twelve thousand men at the mouth of the Rio Grande. On March 3, in America's first amphibious assault, they landed on a beach three miles south of Vera Cruz. Protected by offshore bombardment from American Navy ships, Scott's army surrounded the city by March 15. He accepted its surrender on March 29.

Moving inland toward Mexico City, Scott's men then marched fifty miles to the village of Cerro Gordo. Santa Anna's troops were waiting above a narrow gorge along the route to ambush the passing Americans. However, Scott's engineers saved many lives by spotting an old

Major General Winfield Scott of the United States Army overlooks the harbor in the Mexican city of Vera Cruz. Scott's army captured the city in March 1847 through the first amphibious landing ever made by American military forces.

trail that allowed the American soldiers to circle behind the Mexicans' position. The quick-thinking officers were lieutenants Robert E. Lee, George B. McClellan, and P. G.T. Beauregard, all of whom later became famous generals in the Civil War.

Battles broke out throughout the spring and summer of 1847, with weeks of quiet between them. The Americans continued to suffer from diseases, poor food, and bad water. Scott once had three thousand names on the sick list, with no relief in sight. Recovery took weeks, and sometimes there were too few men to fight.

In the summer of 1847, reinforcements from the

American infantrymen successfully battle Mexican soldiers during the Battle of Churubusco in August 1847.

United States boosted Scott's army to fourteen thousand men. He led three battles in August and September to wear down Mexico's defenses as he continued to pursue Santa Anna. Every conflict cost Mexico thousands of injured and dead soldiers, while their wily leader, using disguises and hiding places, managed to elude Scott again and again.

The final encounter came in September 1847 as the Americans assaulted Chapultepec, the hilltop site of Mexico's military academy. The only defenders were young, untrained cadets who could not do much to stop the Americans, and the attack ended before noon.

America's war with Mexico was finally over. Santa

American troops storm Chapultepec, which was defended by young cadets from Mexico's military training academy. This battle ended the Mexican War in September 1847.

Anna resigned on September 16 and left the country three weeks later. Polk was ready to negotiate a treaty.

The president had sent Nicholas Trist, chief clerk of the State Department, to Mexico on April 10, 1847. Trist had to wait five months for the fighting to end before he could begin his confidential mission to work with General Scott and arrange a peace settlement. When the two men finally met, they disliked each other instantly, and their squabbles delayed progress.

Weeks went by without results. Polk became impatient and fired Trist, who ignored him and continued negotiating with Mexican authorities. On February 2, 1848, Trist and Mexico's acting president,

United States Marines, led by General Quitman, march into Mexico City after Mexican general Antonio López de Santa Anna left the country in September 1847.

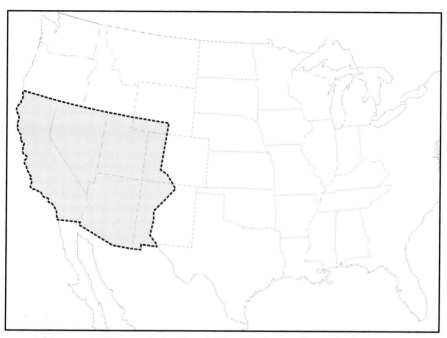

This map indicates the land ceded by Mexico to the United States in the Treaty of Guadalupe-Hidalgo, which went into effect on July 4, 1848. The territory is the dotted area on the left side of the map.

Peña y Peña, met in the village of Guadalupe-Hidalgo to sign a treaty of the same name.

Although he had angered the president, Trist managed to win all of Polk's terms. These included (1) the Rio Grande became the permanent boundary between Mexico and Texas; (2) the United States paid Mexico $15 million dollars for the provinces of Alta California and most of New Mexico; (3) the United States paid off all claims made against Mexico by American citizens, provided the claims had originated before the date of the treaty and did not exceed a grand total of $3,250,000; and (4) the United States recognized prior

This stone marker was the first of hundreds to be installed after the signing of the Treaty of Guadalupe-Hidalgo. They ran along the two-thousand-mile border between the United States and Mexico. The inscription is written in both English and Spanish.

land grants in the Southwest and offered citizenship to Mexicans living in the area.

President Polk accepted and signed the treaty, thereby adding more than a million square miles of land to the United States. This land parcel was the largest territorial gain the United States had made since James Monroe had finalized the Louisiana Purchase. American forces left for home on June 12, after the treaty had been ratified by the United States and Mexico. The Treaty of Guadalupe-Hidalgo went into effect on July 4, 1848.

9

POLK COMPLETES HIS PRESIDENCY

Two of Polk's presidential goals were achieved when the Oregon and Texas territories came under American control, and Polk was eager to pursue his other two major objectives: In fact, by September 1846, he and the Congress had completed legislation that reduced import tariffs and established the independent bank.

Polk had opened the subject of tariffs in his first Annual Message, delivered to Congress by his private secretary on December 2, 1845. Congressmen had called at the White House that evening to say they approved of both his message and his plan. The Walker Tariff Act of 1846 was written by Secretary of the Treasury Robert J. Walker. It was the first of its kind to come from the executive branch of the government.

Tariff bills were usually written by the House Ways and Means Committee. When Polk was on that committee during Jackson's administration, he considered tariffs a decent source of government income. However, he did not want tariffs to be so high that foreign products could not compete with those made in America.

In Walker's bill, tariffs were based on the value of each individual item, not on the total number of items imported in a shipment.[1] There were no tariffs on tea and coffee. The bill had one new feature, which allowed buyers to store imported goods in warehouses until the tariffs were paid.[2] Previously, buyers had to pay the tariffs before they could claim their new goods.

Polk's fourth goal, the Independent Treasury Act, was passed in 1846, within a week of the Walker Tariff Bill. It established a separate treasury, independent of private businesses or state banks, to handle federal funds. All debts to the government had to be paid in gold or silver coin or in federal treasury notes. Polk's independent treasury established a permanent system, later updated, which established the basis for America's current banking system.

A variety of other business crossed Polk's desk. On August 10, 1846, he signed the Smithsonian Act of Organization. It was named for James Smithson, an English scientist who had never visited the United States. Upon his death in 1829, Smithson had willed five hundred thousand dollars in gold to the United States to create an institution for "the increase &

diffusion of knowledge among men."[3] However, he left no detailed instructions, and Congress had to decide how to use the money.

The president, the Cabinet, and regents of the newly formed Smithsonian Institution met one month later to study potential sites for its headquarters. They walked for an hour in the morning heat, but did not reach a decision for many weeks. Polk was an honored guest at a ceremony eight months later to lay the cornerstone for the institution's first building, which would resemble a red brick castle.

Polk personally welcomed visitors to his upstairs office in the White House. A group of Cherokee Indian chiefs came in August 1846 to tell him they had signed a treaty with the government. The tribe had been moved west of the Mississippi River during Jackson's presidency, which caused much bloodshed among their branches. Polk said he hoped the Cherokees could become a ". . . united and happy people."[4]

The president was delighted to meet Kit Carson in June 1847. Carson called with Jessie Benton Frémont, wife of the Army explorer and land surveyor, John Frémont. The three discussed the west, and Carson offered to carry Polk's dispatches to California.

Some visitors received a less enthusiastic welcome. Polk hated the government's traditional patronage system that required him to meet with strangers several mornings a week while they asked him for government jobs. In his diary, Polk questioned why such a ". . . herd of lazy, worthless people . . ." was not ". . . going to work and by some honest calling making a livelihood . . ."[5]

The president reserved a gentler side for children, especially those of dear friends. When William Bass, Felix Grundy's grandson, left college abruptly and without his belongings, Bass came straight to the president. Polk took care of him until his father could be contacted. Polk understood such family difficulties because his younger brother, Samuel, had stayed with the Polks ten years earlier after being expelled from Yale University for taking part in a student riot.[6]

Polk also looked after the family of Colonel Archibald Yell, who was a close personal friend for twenty-five years before his death in the Mexican War. The colonel's son was a student at Georgetown College in Washington, and Polk wrote in his diary that he would ". . . educate the boy, and . . . take great interest in him."[7]

The Polks did not have an expense allowance for an office staff. Polk's nephew, James Knox Walker, became his private secretary, and Walker's wife was Sarah's social secretary. The couple and their young children lived in the White House and shared with the Polks the first Thanksgiving dinner ever served in the mansion.[8]

Entertaining was a necessary and expensive part of the presidency. Although Sarah Polk disliked domestic duties, she managed money skillfully. She and White House steward Henry Bowman worked to control costs. They gave repeat business to merchants who provided top-quality products at discounted prices. Bowman reduced the payroll by hiring extra help for special occasions instead of keeping them permanently on the staff. Bowman was the first steward to have an official role in managing the presidential household.[9]

In 1848, Congress ordered gas lighting to replace candles in the White House. The first lady refused to convert her favorite chandelier to a gas lamp. She was proven wise when the power company turned off the gas at 9:00 P.M. during the first gaslit grand reception. The White House was shrouded in darkness, except for the Blue Room, where Sarah Polk graciously entertained her guests by the candlelight of the chandelier.[10]

"Mrs. President," as the first lady was sometimes called, planned events for visiting dignitaries, government officials, politicians, the public, friends, extended family, and even her husband's political opponents. Taking a cue from former president James Madison, Polk made sure to include his enemies as well as his friends at social occasions so he could find out what they were thinking.

The Polks held public receptions in the drawing room of the White House on Tuesday and Friday evenings. They gave several elegant dinner parties each week, for which the first lady provided excellent menus, varied music, and plenty of lively political conversation. Sarah served a selection of fine wines but no hard liquor. She believed politics and strong spirits did not mix well and often led to noisy disagreements. She also

President and Mrs. Polk (center) posed for this daguerreotype at the White House. Next to the president (to the right) is their favorite dinner guest, Dolley Madison, the widow of America's fourth president, James Madison.

did not offer her guests dancing or card playing, because both activities were against her religion.

A favorite dinner guest was Dolley Madison, the popular widow of America's fourth president, James Madison. The Polks enjoyed her company, and their friendship kept Mrs. Madison in the center of Washington society. The ladies often took long afternoon rides in Sarah Polk's carriage.

The Polks continued to uphold the tradition of New Year's Day receptions. Cabinet members, congressmen, and Supreme and district court judges brought their families and special friends. The Diplomatic Corps arrived dressed in the formal court attire they would have worn to royal palaces. People filled every hallway and corner of the public rooms. Polk spent more than three hours meeting what he once called a dense column of human beings of all ages and sexes.[11]

Except during their first year of marriage, when he entered Congress, the Polks were rarely apart for long, and on those rare occasions they wrote to each other every day. Sarah's letters included two subjects: political news and her husband's health. She worried because he tired easily, as he had done throughout his life.

Sarah Polk refused to receive guests on Sundays. She said it was because of her religion, but perhaps she was trying to give her husband a day off with no questions asked. The president had a cold on May 2, 1847, when he wrote in his diary that the ". . . quiet rest of the Sabbath day is always desirable to me. . . ."[12]

Polk was tired because he spent most of his time at his desk. He needed relaxation and outdoor exercise. Early in his term, he had ridden horseback regularly with Secretary of the Navy George Bancroft. He rode less often after Bancroft left Washington in 1846 to become America's minister to Great Britain.

Before Bancroft's departure, on August 15, 1845, he and Polk established the Naval School in Annapolis, Maryland.[13] It was renamed the United States Naval Academy five years later. All midshipmen, as the students were called, were required to live in Bancroft

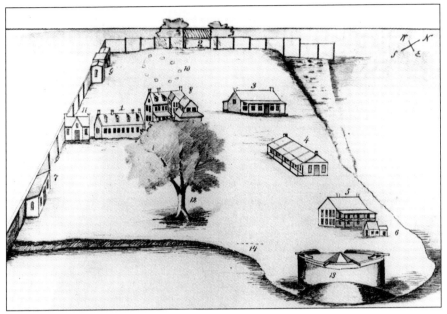

The first buildings of the Naval School, established in August 1845 by President Polk and George Bancroft, secretary of the Navy, are shown in this early drawing. The school was renamed the United States Naval Academy five years later.

Hall, which later became the world's largest student dormitory.

The president seldom had the opportunity to enjoy a refreshing change of scene. However, in late May 1847 the Polks spent a week at the University of North Carolina and were greeted by large crowds. The president delighted in meeting members of his old debate club, the Dialectic Society. They thanked him for sitting for the portrait they had commissioned from the renowned artist Thomas Sully. In July, Polk enjoyed a two-week political tour through Maine and New Hampshire.

On November 2, his fifty-second birthday, Polk made an entry in his diary stating that he wished the last third of his term were over. Within months after taking office, his friends had begun asking whether he would reconsider his decision to serve only one term. He continued to tell everyone he was not interested in another term because he was eager to retire.

On July 4, 1848, Polk attended a ceremony to lay the cornerstone for the Washington Monument. For the ceremony, dignitaries used the same trowel George Washington had used to lay the cornerstone of the Capitol building in 1795.

In mid-August, Polk told his Cabinet he was completely worn out because ". . . my labours, responsibilities, and anxieties have been very great."[14] He had not been more than three miles from his office in thirteen months. Therefore, he decided to go to Bedford Springs, Pennsylvania, for two weeks of rest.

The first lady stayed home with out-of-town guests while Polk traveled with his nephew, Samuel P. Walker, and a Navy surgeon. Once the other guests learned of his presence at the resort, the president had little privacy or time to himself.

Polk relished the country atmosphere of Bedford Springs. He managed to slip away for private walks in the gardens, and twice he climbed a nearby hill. The cool air was a relief from Washington's humidity. Polk took care of himself, made a fire in the afternoons, slept

Mathew Brady took this early photograph, or daguerreotype, shortly before Polk's term as president ended in 1849. Taking this type of picture required the subject to remain still for twenty seconds or more. Polk's postwar fatigue is evident in his expression.

soundly under a blanket, and wrote that the site must be lovely in hot weather. He returned to Washington much calmer and ready to resume his heavy burdens.

The president once called himself the hardest-working man in America, and he was probably right. He was too busy to write in his diary during the last months of his term. On his last day as president, Polk worked all day in his office, meeting visitors, accepting the resignations of his Cabinet, and signing hundreds of government papers. One document created the Department of the Interior. It brought together several smaller organizations that had not fit elsewhere, including the Office of Indian Affairs and the Patent Office.

At sunset the Polk family left the White House and went to Willard's Hotel. Polk and the Cabinet drove on to the Capitol, where Congress was embroiled in an emotional debate over the Civil and Diplomatic Appropriations Bill. Congress could not adjourn before a vote, because the bill authorized funds to run the government.

Polk returned to Willard's Hotel before dawn, where he fell asleep in his street clothes. A committee from the Capitol came at 6:00 A.M., and Polk signed his last official document. True to himself, and conscientious to the last moment, he had finished all his presidential business and had ". . . left a clean table for my successor."[15]

10

RETIREMENT

I am exceedingly relieved that I feel free from all public cares," Polk wrote on March 4, 1849.[1] The next day, the Polks said good-bye to friends who had braved the icy rain to see them off on their journey home to Nashville.

The couple traveled by steamboat and train through Virginia, the Carolinas, and Georgia. The former president waved and bowed to large crowds along his route. He addressed the House of Delegates in Richmond, Virginia, and acknowledged applause from a theater audience in Mobile, Alabama. The weather warmed and felt more like summer as they went south.

They boarded a steamboat in Mobile. Every stop meant bands, speeches, and big meals ashore. Polk appreciated the kind gestures, but he would have preferred to rest on board. Local officials, refusing to take no for an answer, pressed Polk until he consented to their invitations.

By the tenth day of the trip, Polk's health began to falter. He needed peace and quiet and was upset to hear that the city of New Orleans had arranged special events to honor him. Polk knew he could not decline without appearing rude. When he arrived in the city, an elaborate French breakfast was served. Concerned that his queasy stomach might reject the food, he quietly asked a waiter to bring him ". . . a piece of cornbread and broiled ham."[2]

Polk was driven through New Orleans in an open carriage. He was hot, dusty, and tired as he tried to acknowledge the throngs lining both sides of the streets. The mayor insisted the Polks remain in New Orleans another day, because he had invited two hundred fifty people to a dinner in their honor. The mayor implied that their early departure would embarrass the city, and the Polks felt they had no choice but to stay.

By the third week of the trip, Polk was very ill. He was weak and could not eat because of abdominal cramps. He was alarmed to hear that a fellow passenger on the boat had died of cholera. Sarah Polk sent for a physician when they reached Memphis, Tennessee. Dr. Jones advised them to leave the boat and rest at a hotel in nearby Smithland. He remained with them for four days while Polk rallied enough to finish the trip. The one-month journey ended at last. The Polks were overwhelmed by the welcome from the huge crowd waiting on the dock in Nashville.

Polk's health improved after he and Sarah moved into their new home, Polk Place, in April 1849. The house was special to them because it had once been owned by Felix Grundy, Polk's law mentor and friend. They began to remodel, and Mrs. Polk arranged the furniture she had bought in New York the previous summer.

Polk was ill again in early June. Doctors diagnosed his violent intestinal cramps and inability to eat as a case of cholera. His strength ebbed, and he decided it was time to be baptized. His mother, Jane, who still lived in Columbia, hurried to his bedside accompanied by her own minister.

However, Polk sent for Reverend John McFerrin instead. They had met at a camp revival meeting on Polk's birthday in 1833. Although he had been surrounded by staunch Presbyterians all his life, James Polk had cherished a secret devotion to the Methodist faith for almost twenty years.[3] Reverend McFerrin performed the simple baptism ceremony and received Polk into the Methodist Church.

Six days later, on June 15, 1849, James Knox Polk died of cholera. He was fifty-three years old and had been out of office only three months.

After Polk's death, Sarah appointed herself her husband's representative in his absence. She took pride in his belief that the presidency belonged to all the people in the United States, and she considered her home a politically neutral ground for all Americans. Always a skilled financial manager, Sarah oversaw the Polks' properties until she eventually sold them for a tidy profit shortly before the Civil War.

Sarah Polk always enjoyed the company of guests. During the Civil War, she invited both Union and Confederate officers to call on her. She offered gracious hospitality to all her visitors, although she sympathized with ". . . the lives of the people with whom I always lived, and whose ways were my ways. . . ."[4] The Union Army stationed a sentry patrol around her home throughout the war to keep her safe.

In her later years, Sarah Polk's life revolved around her family and her church. She lived in Polk Place, often with one or more of her many nieces and nephews, until 1891. When she died, at the age of eighty-seven, she was buried next to her husband in the garden near the house. Later, the Polks were both moved to a permanent gravesite on the grounds of the state capitol in Nashville, Tennessee.

11

LEGACY

James Knox Polk was a rare president. He stated clearly what he planned to do, achieved all his goals, and retired after one term, as promised. Forty-nine years old when he took office, Polk was the nation's most successful one-term president. He is still the only Speaker of the House of Representatives ever to be elected president.

James Polk had a profound effect on the destiny of the United States. He possessed the vision, courage, and determination to understand that America's western boundary should extend beyond the Mississippi River and the Rocky Mountains. He knew the country must eventually reach to the Pacific Ocean.

Polk's administration added 1.2 million square miles to the territory of the United States. This addition increased the size of the country by more than 60 percent.[1] The new land came from the Oregon settlement, the annexation of Texas, and acquisitions from the Mexican War. Land gained during Polk's administration eventually became all or part of thirteen western states, including Arizona, California, Colorado, Idaho, Kansas, Montana, Nevada, New Mexico, Oklahoma, Oregon, Utah, Washington, and Wyoming.

In 1848, in a special message to Congress, President Polk announced that America's future was secure. His policy, known as the Polk Doctrine, reaffirmed the Monroe Doctrine that had been written in 1823 by former president James Monroe. Monroe had declared that from then on no European colony or dominion could be established on the continent of North America. Polk took the Monroe Doctrine one step further by prohibiting any European meddling in any territorial expansion the United States might undertake in North America.

President Polk went largely unnoticed for sixty years after his death. His legacy was overshadowed by the tumultuous times of presidential giants Andrew Jackson and Abraham Lincoln. Polk's diary was not published until 1910, when five hundred copies were printed. His eyewitness accounts offered new insight into the people and events of his administration, one of America's most exciting periods. The diary clearly conveys Polk's devotion to politics above most other interests.

Every president's place in history is ranked by historians who do not always agree on exactly where to

James and Sarah Polk are now buried in a marble tomb on the grounds of the capitol in Nashville. Their bodies were moved from the garden of their home in the same city.

position their subjects. It is a difficult decision because all presidents faced different problems and changing times. Charles de Gaulle, former president of France, once said, "To be great, you must marry great events."[2] Professor Walter A. McDougall from the University of Pennsylvania said, "Being a great President requires the right opportunities, the right choices, and the right historian."[3]

Historians, including McDougall, all rate James Polk a "near great" president. According to various polls, he ranks between sixth and twelfth on the scale of America's forty-two presidents. McDougall writes of Polk, "He was the greatest conqueror in U.S. history save Washington himself . . . Polk . . . made peace [with Britain, in 1844] and war [with Mexico, in 1846] for limited ends with realistic means. He also kept his promise to step down after one term."[4]

Chronology

1795—Born November 2 in Pineville, North Carolina.

1806—Moved to Duck River valley, Tennessee.

1812—Survived life-threatening abdominal surgery.

1813—Began formal education at Zion Church Academy Day School.

1818—Graduated with highest honors from the University of North Carolina.

1819—Studied law with state senator Felix Grundy in Nashville, Tenn; elected clerk of the Tennessee state senate.

1820—Passed bar exam and was admitted to Tennessee Bar Association.

1823—Elected to Tennessee legislature.

1824—Married Sarah Childress.

1824—Elected to United States House of
–1835 Representatives, served seven consecutive terms.

1827—Appointed member, House Committee on Foreign Affairs.

1832—Appointed member, House Ways and Means Committee.

1833—Appointed chairman, House Ways and Means Committee.

1835—Elected Speaker of the House, served two
–1839 terms.

1839—Elected governor of Tennessee, served one
–1841 term.

1844—Nominated as the "dark horse" Democratic presidential candidate; elected eleventh president of the United States.

1845—Inaugurated March 4, at age forty-nine; signed legislation admitting Texas as twenty-eighth state.

1846—Negotiated Oregon Treaty; signed Walker Tariff Act; signed Independent Treasury Act; declared war with Mexico.

1846—Directed strategic planning of Mexican War.
–1848

1848—Signed Treaty of Guadalupe-Hidalgo.

1849—Retired March 5; returned to Nashville; died of cholera on June 15 at the age of fifty-three.

1891—Sarah Polk died in Nashville at the age of eighty-seven.

Chapter Notes

Chapter 1. Inauguration Day

1. Louise Durbin, *Inaugural Cavalcade* (New York: Dodd, Mead, 1971), p. 57.

2. Ibid., p. 59.

3. Betty Boyd Caroli, *First Ladies,* expanded edition (New York: Oxford University Press, 1995), p. 59.

4. James K. Polk, "Inaugural Address, Section 26," *Grolier Online, The American Presidency,* n.d., <http://www.grolier.com/presidents/aae/inaugs/1845Polk.html> (March 1998).

5. Ibid., section 11.

6. Durbin, p. 61.

7. Ibid.

Chapter 2. The Country Boy

1. Paul H. Bergeron, *The Presidency of James K. Polk* (Lawrence: The University Press of Kansas, 1987), p. 9.

2. Ibid., p. 10.

3. Sam W. Haynes, *James K. Polk and the Expansionist Impulse* (New York: Longman, 1997), p. 4.

4. William A. DeGregorio, *Complete Book of U.S. Presidents* (New York: Barricade Books, 1993), p. 164.

5. George Harris, ed., *Polk Campaign Biography* (Knoxville: Tennessee Presidents' Trust, 1990), p. 5.

6. Ibid.

7. Haynes, p. 9.

8. John J. Farrell, *James K. Polk, 1795–1849* (New York: Oceana Publications, Inc., 1970), p. 1.

9. DeGregorio, p. 165.

10. Frank N. Magill, ed., *The American Presidents, the Office and the Men* (Pasadena: Salem Press, 1986), p. 220.

11. Haynes., p. 11.

12. Betty Boyd Caroli, *First Ladies, Expanded Edition* (New York: Oxford University Press, 1995), p. 59.

13. Margaret Truman, *First Ladies* (New York: Random House, 1995), p. 97.

14. Paul F. Boller, Jr., *Presidential Wives* (New York: Oxford University Press, 1988), p. 89.

15. Harris, p. 9.

Chapter 3. The Congressman

1. John J. Farrell, *James K. Polk, 1795–1849* (New York: Oceana Publications, Inc., 1970), p. 2.

2. Sam W. Haynes, *James K. Polk and the Expansionist Impulse* (New York: Longman, 1997), p. 18.

3. Frank N. Magill, ed., *The American Presidents, the Office and the Men* (Pasadena: Salem Press, 1986), p. 222.

4. Betty Boyd Caroli, *First Ladies,* expanded edition (New York: Oxford University Press, 1995), p. 60.

5. Haynes, p. 21.

6. Farrell, p. 2.

7. Margaret Truman, *First Ladies* (New York: Random House, 1995), p. 98.

8. Ibid., pp. 97–98.

9. Farrell, p. 3.

10. Haynes, p. 16.

11. Ibid., p. 22.

12. George Harris, ed., *Polk Campaign Biography* (Knoxville: Tennessee Presidents' Trust, 1990), p. 3.

13. William A. DeGregorio, *Complete Book of U.S. Presidents* (New York: Barricade Books, 1993), p. 164.

14. Ibid., p. 116.

15. Farrell, p. 4.

16. Ibid.

Chapter 4. The Texas Issue

1. *The Alamo Long Barrack Museum* (Dallas: Taylor Publishing, 1986), p. 13.

2. Ibid., p. 14.

3. Ibid.

4. Ibid., p. 22.

5. Norton, David M. Katzman, William M. Tuttle, Jr., Howard P. Chudacoff and Paul D. Escott, *A People & a Nation*, 3rd ed., vol. 1 (New York: Houghton Mifflin, 1990), p. 374.

6. John J. Farrell, *James K. Polk, 1795–1849* (New York: Oceana Publications, Inc., 1970), p. 5.

7. Ibid., p. 6.

Chapter 5. The Dark Horse

1. Sam W. Haynes, *James K. Polk and the Expansionist Impulse* (New York: Longman, 1997), p. 54.

2. Ibid., p. 55.

3. Ibid.

4. Ibid., p. 58.

5. Ibid., p. 59.

6. John J. Farrell, *James K. Polk, 1795–1849* (New York: Oceana Publications, Inc., 1970), p. 7.

7. Haynes, p. 60.

8. Farrell, p. 8.

Chapter 6. The Road to the White House

1. Eugene Irving McCormac, *James K. Polk, A Political Biography* (New York: Russell & Russell, 1965), p. 248.

2. Rexford G. Tugwell, *How They Became President* (New York: Simon & Schuster, 1964), p. 139.

3. John J. Farrell, *James K. Polk, 1795–1849* (New York: Oceana Publications, Inc., 1970), p. 12.

4. Sam W. Haynes, *James K. Polk and the Expansionist Impulse* (New York: Longman, 1997), p. 89.

5. Ibid., pp. 87–88.

6. *Events in the West, 1840–1850*, <http://www.pbs.org/weta/thewest/wpages/wpgs200> (March 1997).

7. Paul H. Bergeron, *The Presidency of James K. Polk* (Lawrence: The University Press of Kansas, 1987), p. 5.

8. Carl Sferrazza Anthony, *First Ladies* (New York: William Morrow, 1990), p. 135.

9. Farrell, p. 9.

10. Norton, David M. Katzman, William M. Tuttle, Jr., Howard P. Chudacoff and Paul D. Escott, *A People & a Nation*, 3rd ed., vol. 1 (New York: Houghton Mifflin, 1990), p. 368.

11. William Seale, *The President's House* (Washington: The White House Historical Association, 1986), p. 250.

Chapter 7. The Oregon Territory

1. Charles Grier Sellers, *James K. Polk: Continentalist, 1843–1846* (Princeton, N.J.: University Press, 1966), p. 213.

2. Allan Nevins, ed., *Polk, the Diary of a President* (New York: Longmans, Green, 1929), p. 141.

3. Ibid., p. 2.

4. Ibid., p. 19.

5. *Events in the West, 1840–1850*, <http://www.pbs.org/weta/thewest/wpages/wpgs200> (March 1997).

6. Nevins, p. 379.

7. Ibid., p. 42.

8. Ibid., pp. 59–60.

9. John J. Farrell, *James K. Polk, 1795–1849* (New York: Oceana Publications, Inc., 1970) p. 14.

10. Ibid., pp. 14–15.

Chapter 8. The Mexican War

1. Norton, David M. Katzman, William M. Tuttle, Jr., Howard P. Chudacoff and Paul D. Escott, *A People & a Nation*, 3rd ed., vol. 1 (New York: Houghton Mifflin, 1990), p. 367.

2. John J. Farrell, *James K. Polk, 1795–1849* (New York: Oceana Publications, Inc., 1970), p. 11.

3. Ibid.

4. Allan Nevins, ed., *James K. Polk, the Diary of a President* (New York: Longmans, Green, 1929), p. 183.

5. Ibid., p. 207.

6. Ibid., p. 230.

7. Ibid., p. 225.

Chapter 9. Polk Completes His Presidency

1. *The World Book Multimedia Encyclopedia* <http://www.worldbook.com> (March 20, 1997).

2. William A. DeGregorio, *Complete Book of U.S. Presidents* (New York: Barricade Books, 1993), p. 171.

3. *150 Years of Smithsonian History* <http://www.si.edu/smithexb/sitime.htm> (March 20, 1997).

4. Allan Nevins, ed., *Polk, the Diary of a President* (New York: Longmans, Green, 1929), p. 139.

5. Ibid., p. 319.

6. John J. Farrell, *James K. Polk, 1795–1849* (New York: Oceana Publications, Inc., 1970), p. 5.

7. Nevins, p. 208.

8. William A. DeGregorio, *Complete Book of U.S. Presidents* (New York: Barricade Books, 1993), p. 166.

9. William Seale, *The President's House* (Washington: The White House Historical Association, 1986), p. 258.

10. Ibid., p. 269.

11. Nevins, p. 361.

12. Ibid., p. 224.

13. *United States Naval Academy* <gopher://gopher.nara.gov:70/00/inform/guide/400s/rg405.txt> (December 7, 1998).

14. Nevins, p. 340.

15. Ibid., p. 382.

Chapter 10. Retirement

1. Allan Nevins, ed., *Polk, the Diary of a President* (New York: Longmans, Green, 1929), p. 388.

2. Ibid., p. 398.

3. Ibid., p. 23.

4. Paul F. Boller, Jr., *Presidential Wives* (New York: Oxford University Press, 1988) p. 91.

Chapter 11. Legacy

1. Sam W. Haynes, *James K. Polk and the Expansionist Impulse* (New York: Longman, 1997), p. 193.

2. James Goldsborough, "The Makings of a Great President," *San Diego Union*, January 27, 1997, p. B-7.

3. Walter A. McDougall, "Rating the Presidents," *National Review*, October 1997, p. 32.

4. Ibid., p. 34.

Further Reading

Caroli, Betty Boyd. *America's First Ladies*. New York: The Reader's Digest Association, 1996.

DeGregorio, William A. *Complete Book of U.S. Presidents*. New York: Barricade Books, 1993.

Ferrell, Robert H. *Atlas of American History*. New York: Facts on File, 1993.

Haynes, Sam W. *James K. Polk and the Expansionist Impulse*. New York: Longman, 1997.

Judson, Karen. *Andrew Jackson*. Springfield, N.J.: Enslow Publishers, Inc., 1997.

Mayo, Edith P., ed. *The Smithsonian Book of the First Ladies*. New York: Henry Holt, 1996.

Nardo, Don. *The Mexican-American War*. San Diego: Lucent Books, 1991.

Schlesinger, Arthur M., Jr. *The Almanac of American History*. New York: Barnes & Noble Books, 1993.

Seale, William. *The President's House*. Washington: The White House Historical Association, 1986.

Stefoff, Rebecca. *The Oregon Trail in American History*. Springfield, N.J.: Enslow Publishers, Inc., 1997.

Truman, Margaret. *First Ladies*. New York: Random House, 1995.

Viola, Herman. *The National Archives of the United States*. New York: Harry Abrams, 1984.

Wenborn, Neil. *The U.S.A., A Chronicle in Pictures*. New York: SMITHMARK Publishers, Inc., 1991.

Places to Visit

Historic Sites

James and Sarah Polk's Gravesite
Tennessee State Capitol
Charlotte Avenue
Nashville, TN 37243

James K. Polk's Birthplace
James K. Polk Memorial
308 Polk Street
Pineville, North Carolina
Telephone: (704) 889-7145

Polk Family Home
James K. Polk Memorial Association
301 West Seventh Street
Columbia, TN 38402
Telephone: (931) 388-2354
E-mail <jkpolk@usit.net>

Andrew Jackson's Home
The Hermitage
4580 Rachel's Lane
Hermitage, TN 37076
Telephone: (615) 889-2941

Researching James Polk

The Polk Project
The Tennessee Presidents' Trust
216 Hoskins Library
University of Tennessee
Knoxville, TN 37996-4000
Telephone: (423) 974-0662
E-mail <wcutler@utk.edu>

Tennessee State Library and Archives
403 Seventh Avenue North
Nashville, TN 37243-0312
Telephone: (615) 741-2764
Web site <http://www.state.tn.us>

Tennessee State Museum
505 Deaderick Street
Nashville, TN 37243-1120
Telephone: (615) 741-2692

Internet Addresses

Columbia University Digital Library Collection
  <http://www.columbia.edu/cu/libraries/indexes>

**Grolier Online Presentation of the
American Presidency**
  <http://www.grolier.com/presidents/>

Internet Public Library
  <http://www.ipl.org/ref/POTUS/jkpolk.html>

James K. Polk Memorial Association
  E-mail <jkpolk@usit.net>

Library of Congress
  <http://lcweb2.loc.gov>

National Archives and Records Administration
  <http://www.nara.gov>; E-mail <inquire@nara:gov>

National Park Service
  <http://www.cr.nps.gov>

The Polk Project, University of Tennessee, Knoxville
  E-mail <wcutler@utk.edu>

Public Broadcasting System
  <http://www.pbs.org>

Smithsonian Institution: U.S. Political History
  <http://www.si.edu/resource/faq/nmah/political.htm>

Tennessee State Library
  <http://www.state.tn.us/sos/govs/polk.htm>

The White House
  <http://www.whitehouse.gov/WH/glimpse/presidents/html/
    jp11.html>

Index

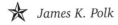